WADE CLARK

SIMPLIFYING
COMPLEX SALES

—————— THE ——————

NEXT STEPS APPROACH

LANDMARC
P R E S S

For general information on our other products and services of for technical
support, please contact LandMarc Press at 936-544-5137, fax 936-544-2207,
or on the web at www.LandMarcPress.com

Design and Composition by Publications Development Co.
Cover design by Publications Development Co.

ISBN: 978-0-9845129-6-6

10 9 8 7 6 5 4 3 2 1

SIMPLIFYING
COMPLEX SALES

Jack

I hope you find this book helpful. Looking forward to working with you.

Wade

I dedicate this book to my wife, and best friend Suzannah. You surprise and inspire me every day. Thank you for your love, support, and encouragement, and for the needed "kick in the pants" you give me from time to time. I love you dearly.

Contents

Preface

Knowledge, understanding, and wisdom—perhaps these are unusual words with which to begin a book about selling, but I want this book to give you additional knowledge, a fresh understanding of the business of selling, and practical tools that will allow you to apply wisdom to increase your sales effectiveness.

- **Knowledge:** The accumulation and retention of facts and concepts.
- **Understanding:** Fitting accumulated facts and concepts together in ways that allow new revelations, ideas, and approaches to develop. With understanding, an individual is just beginning to have the ability to teach.
- **Wisdom:** The ability to use gained understanding practically *to produce a result*. With wisdom, an individual has the ability not to just teach, but also to model and mentor.

Acknowledgments

To my kids—Josiah, Anna, Grace, and Peter—thanks for your love and respect and for the privilege to be called your dad. Thanks to my parents—Tom and Elaine Clark—and to my sister Beth and the whole Cassidy family, I love you. (I miss you Dad.) Thanks to my mother-in-law, Betijean Kennerly, and my father-in-law Dan Kennerly and his kind wife Joyce. And most of all, thanks to my Lord Jesus Christ, to whom I owe everything now and for eternity. May everyone come to know you as their personal Lord and Savior and praise and serve you daily.

I also want to acknowledge and thank the many professionals with whom I have had the honor to work within the accounting profession. You have challenged me to grow and to pursue excellence. Many have helped and inspired me, but some deserve special thanks, specifically: Jody Bieze, Tom Spitznaugle, Russ Dawson, Troy Waugh, Gale Crosley, Alan Deichler, Bill Fingland, Bill Kirkman, Steve Rafferty, Jason Jobgen, Bill Carr, and the dozens of CPAs and marketing and sales professionals I have had the honor to work with and call friends at Ernst & Young; BDO; KPMG; BKD; and Carr, Riggs & Ingram; and through my participation in the Association for Accounting Marketing.

Introduction

This book teaches you how to choose wise and effective Next Steps and make sound business decisions that lead to increased client sales. This book also shows you how using the Next Steps approach will help you manage your growth efforts.

In complex sales, Next Steps are essential because they often become the differentiator between competing firms. Well-planned and executed sales pursuits actually build buyer confidence. This confidence translates into higher win rates for the seller. The seller's challenge is to have a reason for each next step. This may seem evident but my experience in sales management has shown me that next steps are often left to gut instinct, generalizations, and guesses.

Frequently sellers have a next step, but they can't tell you what they expect it to accomplish specifically. This is obvious when the next steps are merely tasks, such as "make a call to . . ." or "follow-up with . . ." Too often when I see these types of next steps and question the seller, it becomes evident that they do not have clear objectives. The seller wants to be proactive, but he or she doesn't know how. They need a road map.

When a seller's next step is simply to have another meeting with the prospect, they are clinging to a hope that frequency of contact will translate into results. While courtesy visits are appropriate, this approach to sales is ineffective and inefficient. It is also discourteous to your buyer because it wastes their time. Sellers following this approach diminish their credibility, and credibility is essential to success. Today's buyers expect expertise and results, and being focused in your approach builds confidence.

Sales are more easily made when a relationship exists between the buyer and the seller. However, building true relationships takes time. Building strong relationships takes a lot of time. In business today, time is not generally a luxury that we have. Expectations are high for quick results, and these expectations are not just coming from the seller's company. Buyers don't want to wait to resolve problems or for an answer to a question. They want quick solutions. But they need help. They need help assessing their situation, and they need help making a wise business decision.

As sellers, we must apply ourselves to truly understand our buyer's situation. We must know where they are in their decision process. And, we must help them systematically navigate their options to make a prudent business decision—a decision that doesn't omit key evaluation points. Doing so takes planning and discipline. Using such a disciplined approach helps both parties. Buyers will have confidence in their decision and will realize value sooner. Sellers will accelerate the sales process and increase their win rate.

A disciplined approach also applies to the growth of your company. Let's look at it this way. Everyone finds loose change occasionally. You may be walking down the street, or getting out of a car, or at the park with your child—you look down, and there is a nickel, a dime, or a quarter, or sometimes even a dollar. I would venture to guess that any one of us could get up right now and go find some loose change somewhere. But, how many of you would be willing to base your financial future on your ability to build wealth that way? Would you get up every day, get dressed, and walk around town picking up loose change to make your living? I doubt it. In fact, I imagine you would find that idea ridiculous. But why?

There are two reasons: First, finding loose change is a random proposition. While all of us would agree we could go out and find some loose change on the ground, we simply don't know where it might be. It is a situation of being at the right place at the right time, and being aware of your surroundings. While it is nice when it happens . . . it cannot be planned. The second reason we wouldn't base our financial future on finding loose changes is that the amount of money each "find" represents is very small. It would simply take too long to accomplish our financial goals.

Unfortunately, many companies and salespeople approach their sales goals in a manner that is not unlike basing their financial future on finding loose change. They are after the proverbial "low-hanging fruit" (a mythical beast that we will discuss later in this book). Many people are caught in the trap of believing sales is simply a numbers game. This places them on a treadmill of activity that is nonstop, inefficient, and exhausting.

You may feel that I am being a little extreme in my example. Perhaps I am. But I would put forward that, if you:

don't have a firm understanding of where your buyer is in the decision process,

don't know specifically where the buyer will or should be next,

don't know what barrier will keep the buyer from moving forward, and

don't have a specific plan to deal with those barriers,

then you are looking for loose change. You are resting your professional success on "hard work," hope, luck, and time. On the other hand, if you:

understand what causes a prospect to begin exploring change or new solutions,

understand the stages a buyer goes through in making a decision,

understand the specific barriers that a buyer faces,

understand and are equipped to deal with these barriers, and

understand how to determine specific Next Steps,

then you are equipped with the wisdom you need to accomplish your goals.

This book is divided into three sections. Section 1, *Business Foundations*, covers two major concepts, the Four Pillars and the Four Objectives. The Four

Pillars (Mission, Vision, Strategies, and Tactics) is a concept that all business professionals should understand, including sales executives. The Four Objectives of sales and marketing explains where sales fits within the process of growth.

Section 2, *The Next Steps Approach*, is where we will examine how relationships and trust impact sales. We will explore the Four Catalysts, which help move a buyer to action, and the Buyer's Decision Model from which you will develop your Next Steps. We will also discuss the barriers that arise in the sales process and some ways to address these challenges.

Section 3, *Sales Management Basics*, provides guidance and sample tools to simplify and focus the management of your individual sales efforts, or those of a team.

Each of these sections will focus on specific concepts, tools, or techniques to equip you to become more effective. I encourage you to initially read these sections in order because the concepts build on each other. Later, you may find individual sections to be good refreshers. You also may wish to extract certain charts or tools for daily reference and use.

Let's get going!

About the Next Steps Approach

As stated previously, the key objective of this book is to help you effectively determine Next Steps in any selling situation. These Next Steps provide you with the ability to gain and maintain forward momentum throughout the decision process. But forward momentum for whom and to where?

Unfortunately, the answer is often—**our** momentum through **our** sales process. Sellers focus on research, prospecting, meeting, qualifying, presenting, demonstrating value, and so on. However, we are not the ones making the buying decision. I think that bears repeating. We are not the ones making the buying decision. So, **our** progress down **our** "sales" process is too often self-serving. We must focus on our buyer, not ourselves.

The momentum we need to build is in the buyer's movement through his or her evaluation and decision process. Therefore, Next Steps is centered on the **buyer's decision process**. Stop approaching sales as something you do **to** a buyer. Your job is to help the buyer make an informed and wise decision. To do so, you must be on the same side of the desk as your buyer.

Yes, as a seller you will accentuate the benefits and positive impact of your product or solution, but don't do this in a vacuum. You shouldn't approach a buyer as if you provide the only good solution, because that is rarely true. You may resist this assertion at first. After all, you have a job to do and goals to meet. And, you truly believe that your solution is the best alternative for the buyer, maybe even the only one.

Your product or service may indeed be the best fit for the buyer; however, the buyer must come to this conclusion as well. To do so, he or she should explore the available alternatives and carefully consider specific concerns. The buyer needs to **know** that he or she is getting the best solution. If so, the buyer will be confident in their decision and more pleased after the sale. However, if a buyer short circuits the buying decision process—either because of impatience or the manipulation of a salesperson—he or she will often have a degree of buyer's remorse. You may have won this sale, but may have lost a potential long-term client.

A true sales professional wants potential clients to make the best decision they can, for themselves and for their companies. Today this decision may be positive for the seller (a sale) or negative for the seller (not buying from us or even not buying at all). Working in the client's interest is always best. Buyers appreciate people who care, and they reward them over time with loyal business.

Next Steps will equip you to help a buyer through the decision-making process. You will become a resource and a partner in the process. You will help your buyer navigate the waters of the decision. In doing so, you will gain trust, confidence, and loyalty. These are essential ingredients in a long-term client relationship. Ultimately and globally, you will shorten the sales cycles of your various pursuits and increase your effectiveness as evidenced by increased win rates.

It is important to pause for a moment. The Next Steps approach of helping a buyer through a decision will only work appropriately if you truly desire the best for your client or prospect. This is not a technique. This is a sales method that must originate from a genuine desire to help your buyer make the best decision they can; whether that decision is in your favor or not. I caution you, if you don't truly have the best in mind for your buyer, your buyer **will** know it.

Next Steps requires you to discuss some issues with your buyer that may be uncomfortable for them, and for you. If you don't approach these issues with true concern for the buyer, then these discussions may backfire. Your tone and approach will be evidently self-serving, and you can kiss the sale, the client, and your integrity goodbye.

I believe that if you are taking the time to study this approach, you are likely a professional. And true professionals care about their clients and prospects. Enough preaching. Let's get down to the heart of what we will be studying.

SECTION ONE | Business Foundations

Think of a time when you met someone who shared a passion of yours, a goal that you were also working toward, or a purpose that you also wanted to fulfill. You probably formed a bond with that person—you felt energy and you felt connected.

Think of what happens when people—members of a church, a community group, or a company—share a common passion, goal, or purpose. You form relational bonds of connection, build energy, and amazing things start happening.

Then why is it that sometimes things don't happen? Why is it that sometimes, rather than seeing amazing progress, you see very little? Or even worse, you see conflict or confusion? The answer lies with the Four Pillars—Mission, Vision, Strategies, and Tactics. When you see little progress being made, odds are it is because of an unclear mission and a nonexistent or poorly defined vision. As a result, the strategies and tactics being followed are poorly formed, disjointed, or even in conflict with the group's goals.

Leaders often do not seem to have a good grasp of these concepts. They confuse terms and seem to lack an understanding about how these four tools fit and work together. Indeed, if you research "mission," "vision," and "strategies" for companies online, you will find these terms applied in many different ways and the concepts are not clearly understood, or consistently applied.

When business leaders don't understand the Four Pillars, their organizations often have activities that are not aligned or are in conflict. In the worst situations, companies lose ground, and, in some cases, fail. At best, the result is mediocre performance or a failure of the organization to reach its full potential.

I am convinced that understanding your mission and a having a clear vision is vital to an organization's growth and success. I also believe it is vital to the growth and success of families or individuals. When the mission and vision are not defined, you are scattered or rudderless in your goals and activities. When known and carefully developed and aligned, it is easy to form strategies, along with supporting tactics. Through these, your vision can be achieved, which will in turn help you further and fulfill your mission.

I would like to ask you to set aside your current understanding of these terms and to entertain the information presented here. My goal is to present these concepts in a new and simple manner. You may find that these concepts click at last. When they do, your potential value as a business leader, advisor, or sales executive can soar.

CHAPTER
ONE

THE FOUR PILLARS

Mission, Vision, Strategies, and Tactics

MISSION

An organization's mission statement should be carefully thought through and crafted. It also needs to be universally accepted and promoted by the organization. To help communicate and promote your mission statement, it should be crisp and concise.

To inspire, a mission must be meaningful. Since they are not time bound, missions shouldn't be fad driven. They should be purpose or cause driven. They should be clear and easily understood. And everyone who joins your organization or works alongside you really needs to connect with that purpose.

Your mission is your overarching purpose. It is your reason for being. Generally speaking, it is the greater good you are looking to accomplish in the world. Missions are generally value based and somewhat altruistic. This is important to consider because everything stems from your mission. Making money is not a mission. But making money can enable you to carry out your mission.

Missions are generally not time based. They should be based on objectives that are enduring, or are of great importance. The following are examples of strong mission statements because they show an understanding of purpose and, in some cases, a charge or cause that extends from or beyond their primary business:

- **Cystic Fibrosis Foundation:** To assure the development of the means to cure and control cystic fibrosis (CF) and to improve the quality of life for those with the disease.
- **American Red Cross:** Provide relief to victims of disaster and help prevent, prepare for, and respond to emergencies.
- **Archer Daniels Midland Company:** To unlock the potential of nature to improve the quality of life.
- **Bristol-Myers Squibb Company:** To help all people live healthy lives.
- **Microsoft:** To help people and businesses throughout the world realize their full potential.
- **NIKE Inc.:** To bring inspiration and innovation to every athlete in the world. The statement continues: "If you have a body, you are an athlete"—they view endless possibilities of human potential in sports.
- **Starbucks:** To inspire and nurture the human spirit—one person, one cup, and one neighborhood at a time. The company also has an environmental mission statement: Starbucks is committed to a role of environmental leadership in all facets of our business.

VISION

A vision is an aspiration towards the future state of your organization—a future state that places you in a better position to accomplish your organizational mission.

Your vision statement is a word picture of your organization, as you desire it to look in the future. It should be detailed enough to paint a picture, but concise enough to be goal oriented and memorable. Your vision statement will describe what **will** (future tense) make you unique. It should list things such as the size of your organization, the scope of your activities, your standing or ranking among other organizations, your geographic reach, your areas of product/service distinction, and so on.

It is important to craft your vision carefully, considering the collective compatibility of the goals you are trying to reach. This requires first going back to and evaluating those goals against the organizational mission; and second, evaluating the goals against each other to make sure there are no natural conflicts. (You would be surprised how often two otherwise "good" goals are incompatible or in conflict with each other.)

Suppose that among a company's key goals was the objective to be recognized as one of the top companies to work for in America. Such a goal would necessitate considerable investments in your people (compensation, benefits, programs, tools, team building, etc.) All of these investments would be good. But what if one of the other key goals of the organization was cost cutting, and a lean operation. Wouldn't there be a natural conflict? I am not saying that the two cannot coexist; however, I am saying that the company would need to proactively examine those natural conflicts and determine specific parameters, a "balance-point." Doing so will reduce the friction between the objectives, and shape more reasonable expectations.

A well-crafted vision statement should be objectives-based enough that you can assess your progress and know when it has been accomplished. Without this element, there is no clear objective or mountaintop for your team to climb. Unfortunately, this is one element most poorly executed in vision statements. Frequently they deteriorate into platitudes such as "be the best," "most admired," "live our values," or "company of choice." While elements of these statements are good, they need to be defined concretely in a way that is measurable.

You may think I am now confusing a vision with a goal. After all, goals are supposed to be SMART (Specific, Measurable, Actionable, Realistic, Time-based). You are on the right track. Ultimately *your company's "vision"* **is** *its overriding goal.* So, a well-crafted vision statement conforms to these standards.

Unlike your mission statement, I believe your vision *should be* time bound. It should be set far enough in the future to be a true stretch, but close enough so that people feel they can almost get their fingertips on it. In today's business environment, I prefer visions that are only about 5 to 10 years out. Any further out, and people start to disconnect.

Strong visions get people engaged. They want to be along for the journey. They want to be a part of the team reaching the mountaintop. So visions should be aggressive and exciting enough that the thought of its achievement inspires your team. Such visions spark the imagination of your team members, as evidenced by creative ideas and new approaches to business. And . . . business leaders please hear me on this . . . this type of fresh participation must be encouraged and readily received, even it if means approaching things in new ways and taking some calculated risks. Fostering such an environment sets the stage for greatness. Stifling it only leads to cynicism among your team and mediocre results.

The exciting thing is that once this vision is achieved, a new vision can be created, one that starts at the current mountaintop and dreams again of new ways to further the organization's ability to accomplish its mission.

As stated earlier, there is a lot of confusion in the marketplace today related to mission and vision statements. Many use these terms interchangeably, which I believe is unfortunate, because they serve different purposes. So, I would now like to explore some examples of vision statements from leading companies. Some of these are expressly given as the "vision statement" of the organization; others use different terms. However, each of these companies express elements of a well-crafted vision statement:

- **The Walt Disney Company:** "To be one of the world's leading producers and providers of entertainment and information. Using our portfolio of brands to differentiate our content, services and consumer products, we seek to develop the most creative, innovative and profitable entertainment experiences and related products in the world." (Mission statement)
- **Ford Motor Company:** "To become the world's leading consumer company for automotive products and services." (Vision statement)
- **Procter & Gamble:** "Be, and be recognized as, the best consumer products and services company in the world."
- **Levi Strauss & Co:** "People love our clothes and trust our company. We will market and distribute the most appealing and widely worn apparel brands. Our products define quality, style and function. We will clothe the world."
- **FedEx:** "Will produce superior financial returns for shareowners by providing high value-added supply chain, transportation, business & related information services through focused operating companies. Customer requirements will be met in the highest quality manner appropriate to each market segment served. FedEx will strive to develop mutually rewarding relationships with its employees, partners & suppliers. Safety will be the first consideration in all operations. Corporate activities will be conducted to the highest ethical & professional standards."

A quick review of these statements shows quite a few of the elements needed in a vision statement. While few of them directly address size, several address the scope of their operations (particularly Levi Strauss and FedEx). Disney and Ford address their ranking in the market. Most address their geographic reach. All touch on areas of product or service distinction, albeit some in a very sketchy manner. Levi's and FedEx provide the best example in that area. As for being SMART (Specific, Measurable, etc.)—Disney, Ford, and FedEx are the best examples.

It is interesting to note that none of these vision statements have a time element attached. This may be intentional, as most of the examples are worldwide leaders in their field. In my opinion, however, adding a time element would be helpful because it would make the vision more tangible. Adding a time element is a way of handing the baton to your team members, and helping them understand that it is their race too.

VISION AND LEADERS

An interesting thing to consider is the role an individual can play in the overall vision of an organization. In fact, it is not uncommon for a dynamic visionary leader to play a proxy role that stands in the place of the vision of an organization. This is not necessarily a bad thing, provided the leader inspires a team spirit and helps the team aspire to greatness. In such a situation, however, the visionary leader must transfer the vision to the upcoming leadership, so that the inspiration of the vision can continue and evolve as the leader retires or leaves the company. You can see examples of this occurring throughout history. Let me provide a couple of examples.

WALT DISNEY

As one of the co-founders of Walt Disney Productions, Mr. Walt Disney could properly be called a renaissance man, artist, architect, engineer, entrepreneur, or business leader. Regardless of what you choose to call him, the man was a visionary. In fact, Walt Disney continued to set and achieve new visions for himself and his company throughout his life. He understood the concept of a vision being your next mountaintop, and he was able to generate loyalty and excitement toward each achievement; whether the vision was to create the first feature-length animated movie or the development of a new type of world-class entertainment park where families could come to enjoy time together. Walt Disney was able to turn visions into magic, and magic into reality. That magic is still felt around the world today.

JACK WELCH

Mr. Welch was the chairman and chief executive officer for General Electric Company from 1981 to 2001. He expressed a goal of making GE "the world's most competitive enterprise." He believed in empowering and rewarding leaders and top performers and in purging low performers, including business units. He thought General Electric should be number 1 or number 2 in a given industry segment and they should abandon the segment altogether if they couldn't achieve that. GE experienced strong success under Mr. Welch's leadership, and he is a widely sought out speaker, business leader, and consultant today.

Vision gives people and organizations a view of what their future could look like. It is a glimpse of great things to come. And you are about to understand another major reason why having a strong vision is so important. Vision must come before strategic planning, because **it is impossible to be strategic without a vision.**

STRATEGIES

How many times in a given week do you hear someone use the term "strategy"? It seems like every time you turn around you hear references to the need for a strategy for this or a strategic plan for that. What is a strategic plan?

A strategic plan is a collection of strategies a.k.a. "approaches" that work together to achieve an overall goal. Some strategies are interconnected and some are independent, but they all must work toward the common objective without conflicting.

Simply put, a strategic plan is to a vision, what a map is to a road trip. It provides a path to reach your destination. This is why you cannot be strategic without having a vision, anymore than you can map out a trip without knowing your destination.

Developing a strategic plan is straightforward in principle. You simply examine your organization's current state and compare that to your vision. You will find there are differences between where you are now and where you want to be—in other words there are gaps. Strategies (approaches) are developed for the purpose of narrowing and eventually closing those gaps. Once you complete the strategies, you will have achieved your vision. So, a strategic plan is nothing more than the collective product (grouping) of strategies to close the gap between your present state and your vision.

Let's explore this further by creating a fictitious company. Let's say you are the CEO of an educational business named New Heights Academy. You offer assistance to students who are looking to go beyond their normal academic requirements to prepare themselves for top-tier colleges. Your business has done very well from its local base, largely based on the teachers you have assembled, but you really feel that the potential exists to take your business statewide or beyond. How might you develop a strategic plan?

First, you must have a mission. Do you know your purpose? At first, the mission of New Heights seemed evident—to promote high academic achievement for gifted students. But is that really all there is to it? You decide to take time to meet with your board members and staff for a planning retreat. Though the discussions you learn something interesting that brings a new picture into view.

All the staff and board members seem greatly concerned about a number of the challenges facing the country and the need to develop students who will engage in engineering and other scientific disciplines to build up a generation of innovative problem solvers. Based on these discussions, you work together to craft your mission statement, which reads:

> "The mission of New Heights Academy is to find solutions to the environmental, energy, and medical challenges facing our country by preparing students to excel in research, engineering, and scientific career paths."

Wow, the electricity in the air was amazing when our team read our mission again. For a moment we forgot that we were only a local school, and now with new determination we began crafting our 5-year vision, which read:

> "Over the next five years, New Heights Academy will extend our presence to all major cities within the state. Our growth will stem from our ability to develop cutting edge curriculum, leverage innovative adjunct professor programs, provide leading edge online training tools, and offer junior intern programs. Our students will be highly sought out by leading universities and will consistently place in the top of their class within their respective programs."

Now you are energized. You see the goal so clearly you can taste it. In fact, you almost feel like you are already there. Are you starting to see the power of well-crafted mission and vision statements? You are now ready to set another meeting to develop your strategic plan. As you think about things, you realize you are no longer intimidated. You feel you understand some of the challenges ahead of you. Now you just need to address them.

You get your team together and review the goals of the organization (as stated in the vision), along with the operational elements of your business. You then build a matrix showing your current state and your future state. This will form the basis for building your strategic plan. It looks something like Table 1.1.

The development of the strategic plan is now simply a matter of looking at the gaps between where New Heights Academy is today, and where it can be. You are now ready to develop multiple strategies (approaches) that you can use to close those gaps. Once completed, you have your strategic plan for New Heights Academy, and your next step is now tactics.

TABLE 1.1: **BUILDING STRATEGY BASED ON CURRENT AND FUTURE STATES**

AREA	CURRENT STATE	FUTURE STATE	STRATEGY
Geographic expansion	One city	All major cities in the state	
Product/Service dominance	Core curriculum	Multidisciplinary curriculum	
Product/Service distinction	Staff teachers	Staff teachers + Adjunct professors	
Product/Service distinction	None	Online tools	
Scope of activities	None	Junior intern program	
Scope of activities	Limited local	Reverse-campus recruiting program	
Scope of activities	Ad-hoc	Alumni support	
Differentiation	Ad-hoc	Alumni progress monitoring	

TACTICS

Like the relationship that exists between mission statements and vision statements, strategies and tactics share something in common. Both strategies and tactics are approaches or steps to be accomplished. The distinction is that strategies tend to be multi-faceted activities. Tactics tend to be more singular or granular. Tactics also are easier to delegate and affix to a timetable.

Tactics are the "to-do" lists of tasks that support the accomplishment of a strategy. This does not make them less important. Well-planned and executed tactics are essential to success. In fact, the battle is won or lost on how well tactics are executed.

Tactics should be thought through, assigned, and given a completion date. Additionally, progress on tactics should be regularly monitored and managed.

If you are looking for a secret to success . . . this is it. Success comes not from knowing what to do, but from doing what you know needs to be done. That is true in business, it is true in sales, and it is true in life; that is as tactical as it comes.

THE FOUR PILLARS—ADDITIONAL THOUGHTS

When an individual or organization truly embraces the concepts provided in the Four Pillars, a unique thing occurs—focus. Suddenly decision making becomes more straightforward because all decisions are weighed against a standard—the organizational vision and mission. This means that the Four Pillars becomes an organizational filter. Some decisions, activities, and expenditures will be filtered out. They simply don't fit. This leads to efficiency and budgetary discipline. So the Four Pillars are not just about what we are saying "Yes" to; they are equally about what we say "No" to.

Before we move on, I want to address an objection that may have crept in during our discussion of the Four Pillars. You may feel these concepts are unnecessary or academic exercises. "Too much theory!" You may point to the fact that there are a number of highly profitable businesses operating today that never directly focus on the Four Pillars. And you would be right.

But I want you to understand that this objection entirely misses the point.

The Four Pillars is not simply about profit; it is about purpose. It is not simply about reaching some objective success measure, it is about creating something that inspires and is enduring. It is about bringing people together, unified toward common goals and by achieving those goals, making a positive impact in the world.

I believe most people want to know that what they do makes a difference. Through the Four Pillars, they can make that difference.

CHAPTER TWO

THE FOUR OBJECTIVES OF SALES AND MARKETING

One of the most intimidating tasks a professional may face is being charged with the growth of business. Whether that charge is the growth of his or her personal book-of-business, the growth of a practice, or the growth of an entire company or firm, the task can seem daunting.

What do you do? Where do you start? An understanding of the Four Objectives of sales and marketing can help.

The Four Objectives provide you with focus. Their emphasis is on the activities that, when accomplished, move you forward with your growth efforts in the marketplace. After all, the market is where the next client will surface. The Four Objectives not only give you direction, they also provide you with the order of your activities.

Let's examine a definition of marketing and a definition of sales.

Marketing is the discipline of promoting your company to a group (a market) of potential clients. It can include any number of brand-building tools or activities (advertising, brochures, websites, events, newsletters, sponsorships, etc.) It is a one-on-many activity.

Sales is the discipline of building individual relationships with potential buyers, identifying their wants and needs, presenting solutions, evaluating and responding to concerns, and securing business. It is a one-on-one activity.

As you examine the Four Objectives, you will see that Objectives 1 and 2 are marketing focused. Objectives 3 and 4 are sales focused. This is because marketing efforts pave the way for more effective sales efforts. Sales can be done without marketing, but it is less efficient. When marketing efforts are well executed, familiarity and confidence builds in the minds of potential clients, and with that confidence comes increased sales leverage.

The Four Objectives are:

1. **Increasing positive brand awareness:** These activities target companies that match the client profile of your firm. They are simply intended to make potential clients aware of, or familiar with, your company and its products and services. Tools include advertising, brochures, websites, printed surveys, and so on.

2. **Providing a positive brand experience:** These are activities designed to connect the people of the brand to the brand and to build credibility and confidence. In professional services firms, these activities include publishing articles, white papers, speeches, presentations, webcasts, and so on. The goal is

that your prospects recognize your team members, connect with them, and gain confidence by experiencing their expertise.

3. **Generating leads:** There is much more to sales than a "numbers game." But you cannot afford to minimize the importance of lead generation. A healthy lead generation program leads to a healthy sales program. And the converse is also true. Lead generation can take many forms: from web efforts, to direct mail, telemarketing, networking, strategic alliances, referral sources, and direct sales efforts.

4. **Executing and managing the sales process:** This is the process of helping a prospect assess needs, evaluate options, consider issues, and make well informed decisions. The remainder of this book will focus on this area.

SECTION TWO | The Next Steps Approach

A **number of years ago,** I was working to establish core sales management practices within a regional CPA firm. Specifically, I was working to implement sales opportunity (pipeline) management firmwide. I thought doing so was critical to growth management, because a pipeline would be a tool to gain a global perspective of our sales opportunities as an organization, and it would provide a glimpse into the details of individual pursuits, allowing us to better guide and manage our efforts.

One of the key data items I required in the pipeline from my sales team was a summary of the planned "next step" on each pursuit. While basic in concept, I found that this request presented several challenges to my team. Most of the time there was not clarity on the next step they planned to take. Too frequently, the next step was simply a statement that they planned to "follow up" with another call or meeting. But, when pressed to explain what they were working to accomplish, there was not a clear answer.

Where do you stand? When you look at your current pursuits, do you have clearly defined next steps? Do you know what each step is intended to accomplish and how it will impact the buyer and move them closer do a decision?

We will explore the issues and challenges surrounding complex sales, beginning with the personal aspects of building relationships and trust. We will tackle directly what it takes for a prospect to move from a state of inactive disinterest to a state of active exploration. We will examine the stages and milestones a buyer goes through when making a major decision, including the impediments, or obstacles they face in that decision. Most importantly, we will chart out an approach to determine effective next steps; steps that will help a buyer advance in their decision process.

CHAPTER
THREE

BUILDING RELATIONSHIPS AND TRUST

There is no question about the importance of relationships and trust in business. When relationships are present, channels of communication are open. Open communication enables both the buyer and the seller to understand each other, leading to better solutions.

Trust, which is foundational for relationships, allows the buyer to act on faith while certain variables are still unknown. The trust a buyer has with a seller provides the confidence needed to bridge the gap between the known (status quo) and the unknown (post-purchase) consequences.

Trust represents the buyer's belief that the seller has his or her best interest at heart. It also demonstrates a belief that the seller has the competence to effectively meet the buyer's needs.

Trust is not cheap, nor is it lightly given. It is established by being tested and proven, repeatedly, in various circumstances, over time. Generally it takes months to develop genuine trust and years to solidify it. Thus comes the rub for sales. Often a seller does not have an established relationship with the buyer; therefore the trust level is low.

You may be curious why the trust level is simply low instead of nonexistent. On this point, I can only provide my opinion. I believe, in general, that people want to believe in others. Like the principle of "innocent until proven guilty," I think most buyers will give a seller (or at least their company) the benefit of a doubt. This gives the seller a foundation to either build on or to destroy. The challenge is that this level of trust does not usually rise to the level needed for a buyer to feel comfortable making a purchase decision. In some cases it is even insufficient to candidly discuss the buyer's real thoughts and concerns.

Even if we had months or years to make each sale, the challenge of building trust would be a hurdle. Normally we don't have months and years to wait for a sale, so instead of a hurdle, we have a high jump to clear. This is especially the case when we are selling services that require the buyer to replace his or her current service provider. After all, the current provider has already had an opportunity to prove him- or herself and to build trust and confidence over time. Even when a buyer is not completely pleased with his or her current provider, there is still comfort and security in the known.

The challenge before a seller is great when there is no established relationship. This calculates into the reason why most salespeople are outgoing and relationship driven individuals. Generally speaking, sales executives are extroverted. They seem to have the ability to develop relationships at a quicker pace. Unfortunately, they also seem to be less detail oriented, tending to sell on gut-instinct, rather than a plan. This can leave them without clear direction, or a good understanding of what to do next and why.

There are three things I would like you to gain from Figure 3.1:

1. **Trust is linked to your relationship level.** At the initial stage of a business relationship, trust is very low. As the relationship grows, so does trust. In the center of the figure, notice the term "borrowed trust." This represents how a seller begins a relationship with a buyer when a referral source has brought them together. In these situations, trust is not actually present for the seller; instead, sellers gain an extension of the trust the buyer has in the referral source. This type of relationship is very fragile. Sellers must understand that they cannot ride on this borrowed trust; they must earn their own.

2. **There is a dual element to trust and credibility.** The dual element is that trust and credibility are built both with the seller's organization and with the seller.

3. **Buyers shift where they place their trust.** Particularly in a service industry, buyers initially trust the seller's organization to meet their needs. (After all if this confidence doesn't exist, there is no basis for business.) However, once trust is established, buyers look more to the key individuals serving them than to the company itself. For all practical purposes, these individuals become the company to the buyer.

FIGURE 3.1 **RELATIONSHIP STAGES AND TRUST LEVELS**

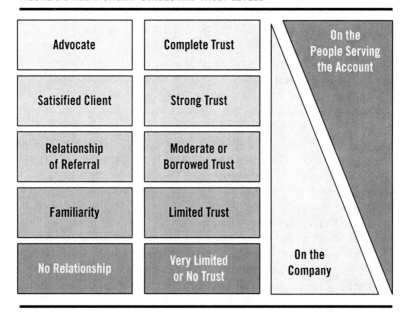

This third point is both positive and negative. It is important to recognize this transition of trust because the retention of the account may begin to rest more on that key individual than on your company. Should this individual mess up, the account could be in jeopardy. Should they leave your company, the client may follow because that individual largely owns the relationship and the client's trust.

To address this risk, I encourage companies to broaden their relationships and service teams with their clients. The broader and deeper your team is serving the account, the more relationships are built, and the greater likelihood the client will remain with the company should a problem arise or a key team member leave. You're creating the proverbial rope, connecting your company to the client. The more relationships added, the more braids in the rope, and the harder it is to break.

HUMAN NATURE: PERSONAL VERSUS PROFESSIONAL

It would be nice to say that in business, business is always the primary concern for the buyer. It would be nice to say, but it would not be true. It is true that buyers must work toward the best solution for their company. They must examine and fully understand their needs and choose the best solution to meet those needs.

However, as a buyer goes through this examination, he or she can be influenced by many personal factors. These factors cause buyers to be selective in their sources of information. Factors influence how buyers filter the information they receive. Some buyers are more prone to personal influences than others. It is up to the seller to understand the buyer, assess these influences, and plan how to respond to their impact on the sale.

A sampling of personal factors is discussed next. But please keep in mind, this sampling is not by any means comprehensive nor are the suggested solutions the only way to deal with these challenges.

PERSONAL CONNECTION WITH THE SELLER

The first and most obvious personal factor is whether or not the buyer feels comfortable with the seller. Do they share any interests or experiences that help them connect on a personal level? In other words, does the buyer **like** the seller? Or better stated, how does the buyer like the seller in comparison to other sellers, or the existing provider?

This factor is one that is broadly understood by sellers, which is a good thing. It is important for a seller, where possible, to make a strong personal connection with the buyer. Looking for areas of common interest or experience will help build a connection with the buyer, as will friendliness and common courtesy (thank-you notes, promptly returned phone calls, etc.).

EGO

Some buyers have strongly developed (some may say overdeveloped) egos. They are very aware of their status in their company. This causes them to expect certain treatment from sellers. Others are simply proud of their personal strengths and accomplishments, and are looking for others to recognize these as well.

I don't recommend feeding a monster, but I do think it is important for a seller to recognize his or her buyer's emotional needs. Some of these buyers have accomplished truly great things. When dealing with a buyer with a strong ego, try to make positive comments on things that are genuinely commendable.

With this type of buyer, it is important to use direct, but open-ended questions. This provides the seller with the information he or she needs. It also will demonstrate to the buyer you recognize his or her control of the purchase decision. (Some buyers are fearful of losing control and may feel pressured.) By allowing the buyer to speak freely and request terms, you are recognizing his or her place in the purchase decision, and you will put the buyer at ease. This does not mean the seller loses influence; instead, this is actually a way to build influence. When you allow a strong buyer to set certain parameters, you are in a better position to stand firm on others.

PAST HISTORY

Buyers are naturally influenced by their previous experiences. If a seller is working to sell products or services with which the buyer has had a bad experience in the past, the seller will naturally have more challenges ahead.

Sellers should carefully examine the buyer's past experiences, and if they sense there may be "baggage," they should tread carefully. The buyer's bad experience may have been with a previous seller's sales tactics. Their bad experience may have been because of the product or service. Or, the bad experience may have been more political within the buyer's own company. Such a situation may have had nothing to do with a seller, product, or service. Instead, it may have come about because of internal politics or conflicts with other team members. The more information the seller can carefully extract the better. The Next Steps process discussed later will naturally work to draw out these concerns.

While the examples given here are negative, in some cases, the buyer's past history may actually work in the favor of the seller if those experiences were positive.

CAREER OPPORTUNITIES AND CONCERNS

A somewhat elusive personal factor is the impact of a purchase on the career of the buyer.

Let's say that there are two companies—Company A and Company B—which are identical in every way but one. They have the same history, vision, strategy, opportunities, challenges, and needs. The only difference in Company A and Company B is their chief financial officer (CFO). Both CFOs have been with their respective company for 5 years. But that is where similarities end. Company A has a CFO whose performance has been outstanding. In fact, this CFO recently has received a raise. Conversely, the CFO at Company B has had a string of failed projects and disappointments. His past 2 years in particular have been so poor that his president has said his job is in jeopardy.

Today, you are going to both companies to sell your service, one that both companies clearly need. The CFO is the decision maker for the services you sell. Ask yourself the following questions:

Will these buyers act differently?

Will they weigh their decision differently?

Will they have different concerns?

The obvious answers are—yes, yes, and yes. But wait; didn't we say that these two companies are identical in every way? Aren't their opportunities and needs the same? Won't your product benefit both companies equally? Again the answer is yes.

Even though the CFOs in our example are charged to make decisions that will best meet the needs of their company, their decision process will be heavily influenced by personal factors. The potential positive or negative career impact of a major purchasing decision can and does influence buyers' purchasing decisions.

There are nonthreatening ways for a seller to ask questions that can uncover whether there may be underlying concerns such as this. But it requires the seller to be both tactful and perceptive. Generally, the buyer doesn't overtly express personal career concerns. (But I have experienced some that have.) Most buyers simply express concerns regarding the importance of this project to be successful, or the urgency that this project not fail. Getting them to express their concerns may simply be a matter of asking: "How important is this project to your department?" or "Are there any internal risks tied to this project that I should know about?" Sellers, please be sensitive when dealing with your buyers.

PRIVATE ISSUES

This factor is one that the seller simply needs to be sensitive to, but probably should not explore. There will be times when buyers are simply preoccupied with issues that are completely unrelated to their job or the decision at hand. Issues with health, relationships, family needs, children, financial needs, and so on can and will from time-to-time distract your buyers and have an impact on their ability to concentrate on the business at hand.

Normally buyers won't express these concerns, but sometimes they may drop hints such as, "Sorry, I've not been available, I've had some personal things come up." or "Sorry, I wasn't able to get back with you sooner, I've been really sick lately." If sellers are sensitive to these potential factors, they may be able to help their buyers (and themselves) by simply offering to provide more space in terms of time, deadlines, and expectations. They may also offer more information or support, such as offering to meet independently with some of the other decision makers in the company, to take the burden off the principal buyer. Please be aware that these private issues often are the most important thing on the buyers mind and heart—over business—and definitely over the sale at hand. This is one of the times that putting additional pressure on the buyer will likely backfire.

DEALING WITH THE PERSONAL FACTORS

You have probably heard the phrase, "It's not personal, it's business." In fact, this line was recently used in a romantic comedy. The character frequently used this line as a way of avoiding the need to look at the impact his business decisions had on other people. Ultimately this character comes to realize that while business is business, business is also indeed very personal. People's lives **are** affected both positively and negatively by their professional lives. If a seller can do his or her part to help the experience be positive, then he or she is doing something of great value, which reaches far beyond the purchase.

In our previous example, our buyer is a CFO whose job was tenuous. While it is doubtful the buyer would reveal personal concerns, an observant seller should pick up on vocal patterns and body language indicating the buyer has a heightened level of stress. It's important for sellers to gain an understanding of their buyer's anxiety related to the decision at hand. If they proactively do so, they can better understand what drives their buyers. At a minimum they can better understand why buyers may feel this decision is high risk. Regardless of whether the seller sees this transaction as routine, if he or she senses the buyer's anxiety, he or she should help the buyer by providing additional assurances, which may be unnecessary for other buyers. This can help build trust and secure the sale.

As a seller, your role is to help buyers with their business and professional needs; however, to discount or ignore personal factors would be shortsighted. I am not suggesting that sellers should jump into personal discussions with their buyers, but they do need to be circumspect and perceptive. Sellers must read their buyers and carefully explore issues they sense could have an impact on the purchase decision or on a satisfied post-purchase experience.

We have now explored the effect of relationship, trust, and personal issues on a sale. These are real factors that should not be ignored. Fortunately, they are not insurmountable. An attentive sales executive can navigate these waters effectively.

A SAFETY NET (FOR THE BUYER)

To be successful in sales, you must develop effective communication channels. It is not enough to create a channel to talk to the buyer. Good communication must be two-way. To be truly effective, the seller must discover things from the buyer that other sellers do not find out, things that only come from a buyer opening up.

At times, we have not had the opportunity to establish trust over time with the buyer. Sometimes, buyers are reluctant to share their true needs and concerns without trust. So, how do we get the buyer to open up to us?

One technique I suggest is to build a "safety net" for the buyer. Let's look at this technique in Figure 3.2.

The circle on Figure 3.2 represents a buyer and his or her current thoughts and concerns. You can see the circle is filled with a wide assortment of random items. These items include hopes, dreams, problems, concerns, relationships, and other areas of importance to the buyer. Some items do relate to the area under discussion (the area of the sale); however, most do not. Buyers think about their company, their career, their family, their friends, and themselves. Each item is

FIGURE 3.2 **SAFETY NET CONCEPT**

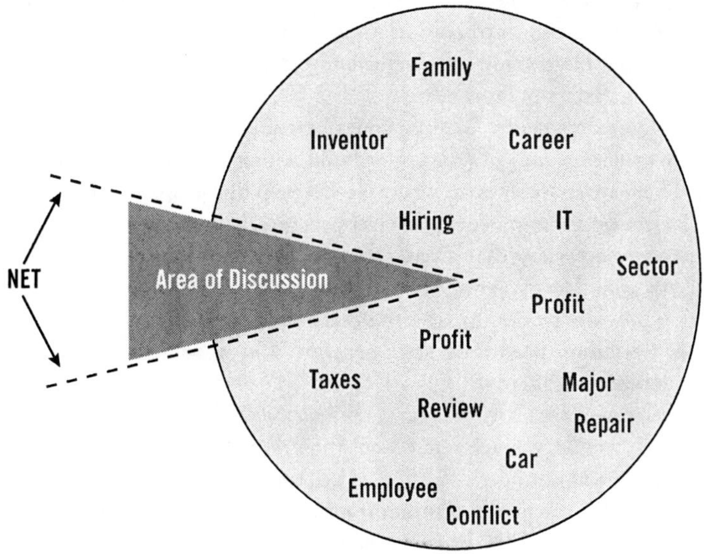

important to the buyer, but not every item is relevant to the discussion. Yet, these items still preoccupy the buyer, affecting their focus, interest, and attention.

When you enter into a conversation where little trust exists, you are obviously at a disadvantage. The buyer is focused on the things listed earlier, and you don't know him or her well enough to know what those things may be. In addition, you don't have the right (yet) to ask too much. Many areas are simply off limits to you now. You haven't built the relationship or earned the necessary trust yet to ask. It is for this reason, I have a disdain for the use of the frequently quoted (and unfortunately used) question, "What keeps you awake at night?" I believe that most buyers think, "It is none of your business!" And, if they think this and answer at all, the conversation would most likely only be a surface-level discussion.

Admittedly, sellers have a number of challenges before them. First, they must work skillfully to gain the buyer's attention and focus, and to keep it. Second, they must begin building a level of trust sufficient to allow buyers to feel secure enough to open up. Third, they must understand that the concerns occupying buyers' thoughts can and will influence their behaviors and purchasing decisions. So sellers must be able to uncover these thoughts and concerns to navigate the decision process.

BUILDING THE SAFETY NET

As you examine the safety net in Figure 3.2, notice the narrow pie-shaped area embedded in the circle. On either side of the pie-shaped area is a border. This border is there to represent what I call the "safety net" we are putting in place for the buyer. Is it always necessary to build a safety net? No. However, when you are meeting with a prospect where a relationship and trust are not yet established, you may find your buyers closed and reluctant to discuss their situation. It is times like these when a safety net can help.

Build a safety net by focusing your discussion and allowing your expertise on a single or narrow area of concern to build your credibility. You may say, "What area? There are so many areas where we can help this prospect." Fair enough. You may be in a position to benefit this prospect greatly in many areas. However, your prospects do not know that. Even if they do, they don't know whether they should place any confidence in you. After all, they get a call almost every day from some solution provider requesting time to discuss their company's situation, so they can present a solution promising great benefits. Why should they open up to you? What makes you different?

The answer comes from how you interact with the prospect on the initial call. If you help your buyers relax and focus their thoughts, you can lead them toward a problem-solving mindset. Safety nets help prospects gain this comfort level and focus. The seller essentially communicates to the buyer that he or she will not pry into areas where the seller is not yet welcome. It is a message that states, "I won't go past certain boundaries."

When a buyer knows the direction a conversation is headed, he or she can stop worrying about what is coming next. The buyer knows you won't ask him or her questions that he or she is uncomfortable answering. Safety nets allow buyers to drop their defenses, which is important, because when buyers' defenses are up, meetings become standoffs not discussions.

Building a safety net is straightforward. Prior to the call, the seller identifies two or three areas in which the buyer may have needs. If a buyer is reluctant to talk, the seller begins building a safety net, as follows:

1. Explain to your buyer that there are a number of areas where you have been able to assist similar companies.

2. Let your buyer know that today you would like to focus your discussion on only a couple of specific areas.

3. Ask for your buyer's permission to explore these areas in depth.

4. Let your buyer know you are willing to expand the scope of the conversation if he or she has something else to discuss.

5. Tell your buyer you don't plan to offer solutions today because you would like to take time to think about their situation and consult with your team.

6. Mention to your buyer that you would like to meet with him or her again to review ideas and recommendations, should any surface.

You may say this sounds more like push selling, not consultative selling. I would disagree. It is simply focused consultative selling. You are not pushing certain products; you are simply narrowing the focus of your investigation today. As your buyer begins to feel more comfortable with you, he or she may bring up other areas. This simply means the safety net is working. It is helping your buyer drop defenses. Remember the purpose of the safety net. It is simply a technique to help closed buyers gain enough comfort so that they can begin opening up to you.

OK, let's place these points in a conversation. Suppose you are meeting with Stephanie Smith, the CFO of a multi-state corporation. This company is a manufacturer of high-tech electronic products. Your company has numerous service offerings that could potentially benefit this company. Early in the meeting you find the conversation to be rather difficult. Mrs. Smith is giving short answers followed by uncomfortable silence. This may be a good time to employ a safety net. The conversation may flow something like this:

"Mrs. Smith, I really appreciate you taking the time to meet with me today. I contacted you because we have several clients in your industry and have found that a number of them are struggling with the same issues.

We have been able to address a few of these concerns with some targeted solutions. Some may be helpful for you also; however, at this point I do not know your company well enough to know if you are facing the same challenges or if our solution approaches would fit.

So, I thought we might focus our conversation today on a couple of areas. And, if it is all right with you, I would like to explore those areas pretty deeply. I am willing to discuss other areas also if you would like, but I thought these would be most beneficial today. How does this sound to you?"

You can see from this script, that this discussion is intended to be comfortable, even somewhat casual. This is intentional because your goal is to put the prospect at ease. You also are reducing stress, because you are showing your vulnerability as well as your strength. In essence, you are laying your cards on the table. Most businesspeople I have dealt with appreciate such candor.

The other powerful outcome of using this technique is that you have gained the prospect's permission to ask very detailed questions regarding the business by limiting the scope to a few principle areas. In general, over the course of a discussion, a buyer naturally begins to expand the 'safety zone' and feels comfortable talking about other issues.

Once you begin discovering information from the buyer in the focused areas, you build momentum toward solving a given concern. Having momentum is useful to the seller throughout the sales process. A skilled salesperson should be adept at initiating and maintaining momentum through the buyer's decision process. Let's closely examine this.

THE IMPORTANCE OF INITIATING MOMENTUM

Did you know that some of the laws of physics apply to sales? Newton's first law of motion essentially states that an object at rest tends to stay at rest and an object in motion tends to stay in motion. This is the case unless or until an external force acts on that object.

Have you ever met a prospect that didn't really feel the need to do anything? You probably had a difficult time moving that buyer to action. Conversely, if you have dealt with a prospect that is urgently trying to solve a problem, he or she is usually not open to waiting until you are ready to help.

Sounds similar doesn't it? Newton's first law of motion is alive and well in sales. This is an important concept for two reasons. First, as a salesperson you need to learn how to apply a force to prospects who are at rest. If you don't, they will just stay at rest. Second, once you get a prospect or client into motion, he or she will tend to stay in motion. In other words, you have created momentum. This momentum, if leveraged properly, can be a salesperson's best friend.

The next section of this book deals with forces that place our prospects into motion. I call them the Four Catalysts. Afterward, we will learn how to leverage the momentum and to assist our buyers through their decision process.

CHAPTER
FOUR
THE FOUR CATALYSTS

I t is important to understand that in most sales situations, the seller is initially meeting with a prospective buyer who is at rest or in status quo mode. This does not mean the prospect is fully satisfied with the current situation, but it does mean that any stress or pain is not currently acute enough to move the prospective buyer to solve the problem. This is particularly the case when the problem or challenge is large, complex, or has a high cost attached. I use the term cost rather than price, because many costs are not monetary. Time, risk, career impact, and relational impacts are all additional cost factors in a large or complex sale.

When a prospect is in status quo mode, he or she essentially has the mindset of "why change?" or "I don't want to deal with change!" When dealing with a prospect in status quo mode there are four principle forces that possess the potential of moving that person from status quo to an investigative mindset. These four items are effectively catalysts.

Merriam-Webster's second definition for catalyst states that a catalyst is "an agent that provokes or speeds significant change or action." Sounds like just the ingredient we need for moving a prospect out of status quo mode. So, let's explore the Four Catalysts:

Catalyst 1: Desire
Catalyst 2: Discovery
Catalyst 3: Dissatisfaction
Catalyst 4: Driver

CATALYST 1: DESIRE

Desire is probably the best catalyst a seller can leverage because it is a positively charged catalyst. Essentially, desire is an emotion that is attached to your prospects' wants, wishes, goals, and dreams. If your prospects were able to do whatever they wanted, they would pursue or purchase whatever it is that they desire most.

Unfortunately, for a variety of reasons, our prospects can't always act on their wishes, and the items or solutions they desire are put on hold. Often when this happens, buyers attempt to dampen their desires and emotionally disconnect or distance themselves from what they want; after all, they can't move forward now. So, why dwell on it.

CATALYST 2: DISCOVERY

Discovery is similar to desire in that it is generally a positive catalyst. Many times prospects are not looking for a solution to a problem, simply because they aren't aware a solution even exists. This is why prospects may say they are perfectly satisfied with their existing service provider—they are unaware of other options. They don't know what they don't know; so, they aren't looking. When prospects discover a product, solution, or opportunity that is new, they can quickly develop a desire for that solution.

A salesperson should not make assumptions that their prospects are aware of all solutions. Frequently prospects are indeed ignorant of many of your company's available options. It may be a simple matter of explaining or asking them, "Are you aware that . . .?" This could awaken their desire because you have helped them discover a new solution.

CATALYST 3: DISSATISFACTION

I don't think much time needs to be spent on this item because it is the classic area most salespeople investigate, or perhaps even exploit. What is the client's pain? What is he or she not receiving? How is the current solution unsatisfactory?

Most prospects have some areas of dissatisfaction. This is even the case if a solution is in place. Remember, there are almost always areas that can be improved.

If these points of dissatisfaction become more prominent, frequent, or unbearable, the buyer will naturally begin to look for ways to ease the pain. He or she also may be prompted to action when needs or circumstances change, and the points of dissatisfaction with the current solution become more of a hindrance. Savvy salespeople can use the Desire catalyst to bring the pain of the Dissatisfaction catalyst to the forefront, again initiating momentum.

CATALYST 4: DRIVER

The fourth catalyst is more external than internal. This catalyst represents actions the prospect must respond to due to external forces. These external forces can be within a company, such as mandates from management. Or these forces can be completely outside the company. This catalyst includes such things as industry trends, government regulation, competitive forces, product life cycle, and so on. These are things prospects can ignore only at their own risk and, at times, great expense.

It is important to note, however, that buyers may not be aware of all external drivers. Informed sellers can bring challenges to the prospects' attention respectfully.

THE CHALLENGE—STATUS QUO ▬▬▬▬▬▬

Let's explore these catalysts a bit further. Figure 4.1 illustrates a prospect resting in status quo mode, with the mindset "why change" or "why go through the hassle."

When you begin meeting with a prospect in a status quo mindset, you will be unsuccessful at selling unless you move the prospect out of his or her state of rest. To do so, use the Four Catalysts.

Let's look at an example. A seller goes to a prospect with high hopes of a new opportunity. You prepare for the call, but the meeting concludes with little visible opportunity. The prospect is happy with his or her current situation.

I can't tell you how many times I hear people come back from meetings and say something like, "Yeah, It was a really good meeting. We got to tour their plant and talk about some upcoming initiatives. But, right now they are with _____ and they are pretty pleased. This is going to be a long-term pursuit."

or

"The meeting was OK. We met with their CFO. We had a pretty good conversation, but there is nothing there right now. Let's put them on our mailing list. We'll try to follow up with them next year to see if things change."

There is nothing wrong with longer-term pursuits. Many times your best prospects will fall into this category. And yes, there are times when there appears to be no immediate opportunity. My personal take is that there are frequently opportunities present. You simply may not have built the trust, or asked the right questions, to uncover those needs. The Four Catalysts provides a solid framework for these meetings and also for follow-up activity.

Most of the time, I have found that sellers either don't follow up from here, or they don't know how to proceed from here. They also frequently procrastinate on

FIGURE 4.1 **PROSPECT IN STATUS QUO**

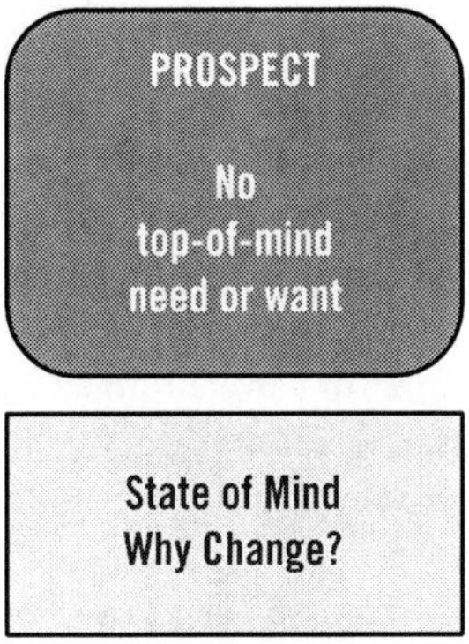

PROSPECT

No
top-of-mind
need or want

State of Mind
Why Change?

any further contacts (touches) with the prospect, because they don't have a plan. They don't know what to do.

I have taught sales to professional service providers, and I have asked them how long it will take them to follow up with a prospect when there was no immediate opportunity. (Then I ask them to be candid and give me **reality** not just what they know they **should** do.) Some tell me they will follow up in about six months, but most say a year. Unfortunately, I suspect that in real life, most of them don't even follow up that frequently, if at all. After all, it is very uncomfortable to call on companies when you feel they don't want your help.

At this point, we continue to work to build relationships and credibility with the prospect (so that he or she will open up to us), and we keep working to better understand and respond to their needs and wants. Therefore we will use both marketing and sales approaches.

I think understanding this may actually ease some pressure on nontraditional sellers (such as professional service providers like CPAs and consultants) because the expectation of "Where is the sale?" is reduced. They can focus on building relationships, trust, and credibility and place their active attention on discovery—a skill most professionals are fairly good at.

However, if we extend our follow up with prospects to only once or even twice a year, our ability to build relationships and trust is significantly hindered. Essentially we are almost starting from scratch each time. We must establish regular contact with our key prospects, but do so in a way that adds value and builds trust. Let's see how the Four Catalysts help with this.

LEVERAGING THE FOUR CATALYSTS

I once worked with a talented sales executive out of Cincinnati who coined a term that I really like. We were in a group meeting, and he was talking about sales pursuits when you meet with a prospect and there is no immediate need. He was asking a question. How can we deliver value and build our relationships when there is no immediate opportunity? He asked, "How do we fill this 'wide area of nothingness'?"

I just love that term. A "wide area of nothingness" (or WAN for our more IT-focused friends) accurately describes how many sellers treat their long-term pursuits. There is a void they work to fill, but they struggle to know how to fill it.

The best way to fill the WAN is to couple relationship development with the Four Catalysts. Keep in mind our overall objectives. First, we truly want to build a relationship with our prospect. As we do, we must develop knowledge and trust. Second, we must deliver value. This is where the Four Catalysts come in (see Figure 4.2).

In the WAN, we should definitely make sure our prospects are receiving any relevant automated marketing material. If your company issues newsletters,

FIGURE 4.2 **INTRODUCING THE FOUR CATALYSTS**

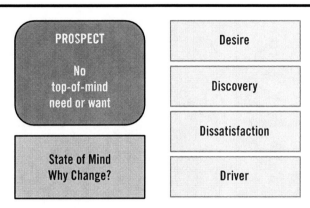

they should be on the mail list. If you offer seminars, webcasts, or mixers, they should be invited. If you monitor news about your prospects, you should send clippings when you see a story about them. All these standard marketing touches begin to build a connection between you and your prospect. But they are not enough. Trust isn't built by mail, or online; it is built personally through one-on-one interactions. If you want to progress with the prospect, you will need to learn about him or her and the company. This is where the Four Catalysts come in.

I would recommend that you determine a contact schedule with your prospects that gets you into direct personal contact with them every two months (six times a year). Not all have to be face to face. Some phone interaction is fine. Email however does not count; it is not interactive. Email can't replace personal interactions.

Your objective in these interactions is to build a dossier on the prospect. A dossier is a detailed file with notes on your prospect. The objective of the dossier is to help you to gain a strong picture of your prospect's situation, goals, challenges, structure, and so on. Four items crucial to include in the dossier are the Four Catalysts.

As you work to build an understanding of your prospect's business, desires, items you can help them discover, points of dissatisfaction, and issues driving the business, you will be able to better advise them. You will have a clearer and more comprehensive picture of their situation. This may help you better understand what may move the prospect into action, which can help you initiate momentum.

The exciting news, you now have a strategic way to fill the WAN. You will have a purpose for meeting with your prospects personally six times a year. You will be meeting to discuss issues surrounding the Four Catalysts.

Now, the fact that we have a business purpose for meeting with the client should not detract from the fact that these meetings should be as much about relationship development as they are about information discovery. So I recommend limiting your discovery process to one of the catalysts per discussion.

FIGURE 4.3 **INTRODUCING THE FOUR CATALYSTS**

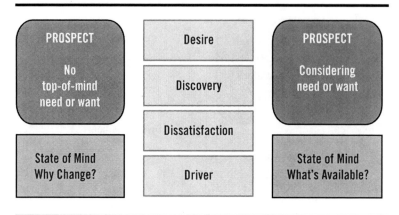

For example, perhaps you begin by meeting with your contact at his or her office and discussing business strategies, goals, and objectives, and so on (Desire).

A couple of months later, you may set up a lunch to share some information you feel may benefit the company (Discovery).

A couple months later, you invite the prospect to your office to review some industry trends and benchmarks. During that discussion, you ask about how the prospect anticipates those trends affecting their business (Driver).

A couple months later, you invite the prospect to a social (Pure relationship development).

A few months later you invite the prospect to play golf. You discuss how satisfied he or she is with existing service. Could the prospect change or improve anything (Dissatisfaction)?

As you can see, these meetings are ways of prompting thought and discovery around the four principle items that have a tendency to move prospects out of status quo and into a status of inquiry. It is not that they are now ready to buy. You simply want them to ask themselves a question about whether or not they should find out more, or look at alternatives, as shown in Figure 4.3.

ADDITIONAL MARKETING VALUE OF THE FOUR CATALYSTS

One additional way in which the Four Catalysts can be leveraged is with direct marketing. When you are developing a direct mail or email piece, you should consider the Four Catalysts as you are developing the content.

Be systematic. Develop mailers that stir up thought around your prospect's goals and desires. Develop mailers (or email alerts) that inform buyers of opportunities they likely are not aware of. Carefully and tactfully develop mailers that touch on pain points. And consider more news-oriented mailers that inform your prospects of competitive, industry, or regulatory trends that could impact their business. When you leverage the Four Catalysts, you are working to move prospects out of a state of rest and to put them into motion—you are initiating momentum.

Table 4.2 provides a list of the types of questions you may ask when exploring the Four Catalysts with your prospect.

These questions are just samples. They are written to illustrate the method of discovery I encourage around the Four Catalysts. Sellers should examine these questions to understand their intent. They should then craft their own questions that center on the Four Catalysts, but that revolve around the solution areas they represent to a buyer.

I use the phrase "craft their own questions" intentionally. The most effective questions and phrases I use in the sales process are a result of introspection and adjustment over time. Generally, the first time I ask a question or state a position, it is not as effective as I intend. Over time, as I adjust the words, phrasing, and tone of these questions, something magical occurs—the question begins to have an impact on the buyer. A hard-hitting question comes across more softly. It is received better by the prospect, and it generates more detailed responses. I do not believe in scripts; I believe in true conversations. However, there are questions and positioning statements that revolve around the solutions I deliver. In those cases, carefully honed phrasing is very beneficial.

The more instinctive a salesperson becomes with questions around the Four Catalysts, the more effective they will become. Buyers can sense when the person they are speaking to is uncomfortable, and that keeps them in their protective shell. However, when a seller becomes comfortable with their questions, and the conversation becomes more natural, the pressure drops, as do the barriers. You will learn more, and the buyer will become more involved in the process. Then the Four Catalysts will trigger the buyer's natural desire to explore the seller's options that may be in his or her best interest. As this occurs, buyers begin their move into the Buyer's Decision Model . . . our next topic.

MARKETING CYCLE VERSUS SALES CYCLE ▪▪▪▪

When a prospect is affected by one or more of the Four Catalysts, it drives a shift in that person's mindset. Questions begin to form in the individual's mind, and he or she sets out on a formal, or informal, quest to get the answers. This is the point when the prospect moves into the buying cycle. It is also this point when the seller shifts from marketing to sales.

I want to extend our examination on the differences between marketing and sales. Specifically I want to address the differences between the marketing cycle and the sales cycle.

TABLE 4.2: **QUESTIONS TO EXPLORE THE FOUR CATALYSTS**

DESIRE	DISCOVERY	DISSATISFACTION	DRIVER
What are your business growth goals?	Where do you typically look to identify new approaches or ideas?	Overall how satisfied are you with the solution you have in place?	What items do you feel your executive team or board really want to see accomplished?
What are your plans for geographic expansion?	What solutions have you explored to deal with _____?	What is working really well for you, with your current solution (or provider)?	Have you been given any direct charges as high priorities?
What changes are you looking for in terms of competitive position in the marketplace?	How well would those alternatives work for your business?	If you could improve something, what areas might you work to improve?	What industry trends do you see impacting your ability to stay competitive and profitable?
What will define success for your business over the next 5 years?	As you have looked at this challenge, have your explored utilizing _____?	Why are these areas the ones that you would focus on for improvement?	Are there any process or technology gaps where you see your business falling behind?
What strategic objectives are you pursuing?	I recently read that one of your competitors tried utilizing _____, What are your thoughts?	Some companies we have spoken with have had frustrations with _____. What have you experienced on that front?	Have you had any issues that have resulted in production slowdowns or stops?
What are your personal goals as it relates to your business over the next couple of years?	Were you aware of the _____ approach to this challenge?	Have there been any service or communications challenges with your current provider?	What regulatory issues are you dealing with now, or do you foresee in the near future?
What is your exit strategy or succession plan?	I was thinking about our conversation the other day, and was reminded of _____. What have you heard about this?	What changes might you make in the client service team assigned to your account?	What competitors do you have the most concerns about?

I have spent the majority of my career working with and within professional services firms—with CPA and advisory firms to be specific. Within my industry, long-term relationships are the norm. In fact, I recently read that the average client stays with his or her present firm for an average of 12 years. You would probably not be surprised to hear that when people describe the sales cycle in my industry, they refer to it as being excessively long, generally years in length. I will not argue the point that many times it can take years between the time a firm identifies a potential prospect and the time it has an opportunity to bid on some work. However, I do contend that during the majority of this time, the firm was not truly in the "sales cycle" but instead was in the "marketing cycle." I believe this distinction is important because the purpose of the marketing cycle is different from the purpose of the sales cycle. Extending from the Four Objectives listed earlier, there are four purposes to the marketing cycle. To build:

- Awareness of your company, its products, services, and solutions
- Relevance of your services and solutions in the mind of the buyer
- Connections between your company's people and the buyer
- Credibility and a positive impression of your people in the mind of the buyer

The transitional nature of the Four Catalysts helps build a bridge from the marketing cycle to the sales cycle by facilitating the movement of the buyer into a solution exploration stage (in other words into window shopping mode.) The buyer's purpose and plans shift, and with it the marketing cycle shifts into the sales cycle.

The purpose of the sales cycle is simply to assist the buyer in his or her search, evaluation, and solution choice to his or her want or need.

Why am I making such a big deal about the difference between these two cycles? What difference does it make? Aren't many of the activities we are doing similar in both the marketing cycle and the sales cycle?

These are fair questions. There are many activities that take place throughout both the marketing and sales cycle. It is important to realize that the mind and purpose of the prospect has shifted. This simple fact is paramount to the activities you do and to the intensity and pace of those activities. Therefore, a buyer's shift from the marketing cycle to the sales cycle should trigger a corresponding change in the seller's behavior and intensity.

PROBLEMS IN CONFUSING THE TWO CYCLES

A PASSIVE APPROACH

Some professionals, who think the sales cycle in their industry is long, begin by passively approaching the market. They think their job in marketing and sales is simply to inform prospects about their company and services as well as build relationships. Then they wait . . . and they wait some more. They essentially think, as long as they stay in contact with the prospect, eventually they will be at the right place at the right time and they will be successful. Actually, many salespeople don't really believe that **their** actions can influence the time length of the sales cycle; so, they think, "Why bother?"

Does this really happen? Unfortunately, yes. In the extreme, I have worked with professionals who have passionately argued that they don't need to have named prospects. These professionals told me: (1) They were active in industry associations, networking, and speaking opportunities; and (2) Taking time to identify prospects was not beneficial because they "never know who will call or what opportunity will arise." They said most of their new business each year comes from sources they had no idea existed the previous year.

I hope you see the problems with their logic. If this were an isolated instance, I wouldn't even address it. But I fought this battle more than once, and I have found that in certain industry niches (particularly ones where industry trade associations and networking are strong) a number of professionals have this misguided mindset. Somehow they think proactively identifying and working with named prospects is unproductive. They consider these two activities mutually exclusive.

When working with salespeople with this type of mindset, I try to get across three points. First, I explain that things can be done to assist a prospect in moving toward a buying decision. Second, I help them understand that these activities are not mutually exclusive; that they can and should strategically pursue named prospects while still responding to opportunities that present themselves. Third, and most important, I explain that by approaching business development passively as they currently do, they will not build their desired client base strategically. They will be left with the luck of the draw.

APATHY

The second problem that can arise from misunderstanding the difference in the marketing cycle and the sales cycle is apathy. When I say apathy, I don't mean the professional doesn't want or care about the sale. Usually he or she cares a great deal; however, **the seller may lead the prospect to believe that he or she doesn't care**. This is because responsiveness in client communications and requests are too slow. At times, responsiveness can be downright embarrassing. This is because the sellers think they have time. After all, the "sales cycle" is long in our industry, they think, "What difference will another week make?"

When a prospect shifts from the marketing cycle to the sales cycle, that prospect's timeline for a solution also shifts in a dramatic way. This is an important concept for salespeople to understand. In professional services, my experience is that when a prospect enters into the buying process (sales cycle), he or she or their company generally makes a decision in two weeks to three months. This is a big difference from years to indefinite. This is critically important to understand because it relates back to the Four Catalysts. As you move a prospect from the marketing cycle to the sales cycle by using the Four Catalysts, you are not just taking the next sales step, you have dramatically influenced the potential time to revenue.

CHAPTER
FIVE

THE BUYER'S DECISION MODEL

I t is time to examine the stages, milestones, and barriers that buyers go through as they seek and assess a solution to their problem or need. We will start by exploring the four stages a buyer goes through. In the next section we will study the barriers that a buyer must overcome to advance their decision. As we progress through these two sections, we will construct a Buyer's Decision Model that can be instrumental to your sales success.

THE FOUR STAGES

The first step in building the Buyer's Decision Model will be to plot the four stages a buyer goes through, when making a complex buying decision. I will portray these stages as four boxes with a gap between each stage (Figure 5.1).

Each stage of the buyer's decision process serves a distinct purpose. Sellers must learn to recognize each of these stages, so they can determine how to assist their buyers to advance in their decision.

STAGE 1—WINDOW SHOPPING

As you recall, the purpose of the Four Catalysts is to help move a prospect from status quo and an attitude of "why change" to the point where he or she begins to explore potential solutions or new alternatives. When this occurs, the buyer enters into a buying stage characterized by exploration and curiosity. The buyer is trying

FIGURE 5.1 **THE FOUR STAGES**

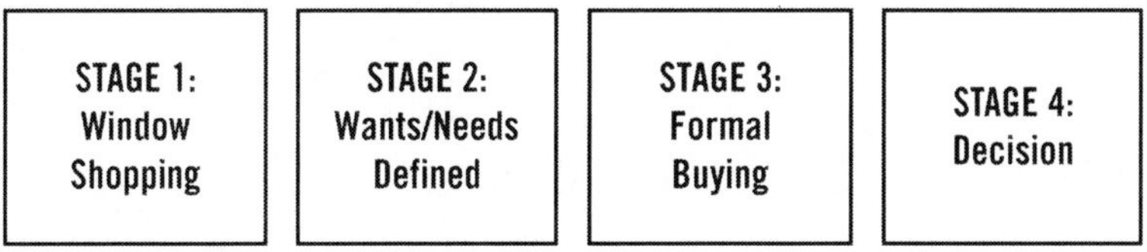

STAGE 1: Window Shopping	STAGE 2: Wants/Needs Defined	STAGE 3: Formal Buying	STAGE 4: Decision

to understand what options and alternatives are available in the marketplace. You are familiar with this stage because it is commonly called window shopping.

In the Window Shopping stage, buyers educate themselves about solutions and their associated capabilities, features, options, and costs. They also are trying to learn about the solution's quality, effectiveness, success rate, ease of use, and so on. The depth at which a buyer explores options and the time spent in this stage is dependent on variables, such as the buyer's personality type, the relative importance of the decision, and the investment required.

Salespeople must recognize the importance of the Window Shopping stage and not rush buyers through it. Buyer education is critical to satisfaction post sale. If buyers don't investigate options, they could regret the decision post sale if another alternative presents itself that could have better met their needs or requirements.

When prospects are in the Window Shopping stage, they are **not** ready to purchase. Let me repeat myself. When prospects are in the Window Shopping stage, they are not ready to purchase. Let's personalize this: Suppose you are driving to a client one afternoon and your car begins to stall out. You don't break down, but you have to pump the gas a few times to get the car to run properly. As you drive to the client meeting, you begin thinking about your car. You have been pouring more money into it over the last year . . . there is also that dent in the back quarter panel where your son backed into a post. You think . . . maybe it is time to get a new car.

That evening as you head home you pull into a dealership just to see what is out and what things cost. As you glance around the lot, up walks a man in khakis and a polo shirt smiling very big. (Oh, great, you think. Please leave me alone!) Of course the man is a salesperson for the dealership, and as you talk you discover he is actually quite nice and knowledgeable. However the salesperson is trying to see what he can do to get you in this car **today**. If this salesperson persists in pushing you toward a decision, you will not only be frustrated, but you may chose **not** to deal with this dealership when you **are** ready to buy. You may even decide to wait on the decision altogether because you don't want to go through the hassle.

Please remember the Window Shopping stage serves a purpose. There are several other stages and barriers buyers must go through before they are ready to buy. In other words, don't become the car salesperson in the example. Don't try to rush a buyer toward a decision.

STAGE 2—WANTS/NEEDS DEFINED

The next stage a buyer goes through is one where he or she begins to formulate a solution. This stage is called Wants/Needs Defined. The overall objective of this stage of the buyer's decision process is to develop a requirements and wishes list. This listing may be formally developed into a solution requirements document, or it may simply be a figurative list in the buyer's mind.

This requirements or wishes list (whether formal or not) is the seller's best tool in meeting a buyer's needs. A significant amount of time should be spent exploring the buyer's needs, wishes, and requirements, and as well as the needs, wishes, and requirements of any additional end user.

There are numerous questions that could be asked at this stage. Here are some important areas to explore:

- What issue is the buyer trying to solve? What need is he or she trying to meet?
- What prompted the buyer to begin seeking a solution **now**?
- What would a successful solution look like? What is success? What is ideal?
- What solutions has the buyer explored in the past? What worked? What didn't?
- What challenges has the buyer faced with previous solutions? With previous providers?
- What time frame is the buyer trying to meet? Is there a hard deadline?
- How much is the buyer seeking to handle internally versus outsourcing?

In a competitive situation, the seller's understanding of the buyer's solution requirements is the best opportunity to differentiate a solution from competitors. If you, as the salesperson, delve deeply into the hard solution requirements and also into the soft, more service-oriented requirements, you should be able to outline two or three additional solution requirements. These additional requirements can become significant differentiators between you and your competitors. **In many cases you will be the only competitor aware of and meeting these additional requirements, thus giving you a competitive advantage.**

STAGE 3—FORMAL BUYING

Once a buyer has explored available options (Window Shopping) and determined possible solutions (Wants/Needs Defined), he or she is ready to move into the next buying stage Formal Buying.

The purpose of the Formal Buying stage is for the buyer to request and evaluate the information needed to make a decision. Therefore, the primary test to see if a buyer is in the Formal Buying stage is if he or she is asking for a bid or proposal. If you receive a Request for Proposal (RFP) from a prospect—you can be assured the company is in the Formal Buying stage. (Now, just because a company is in the Formal Buying stage doesn't necessarily mean that you are as a seller—this is important—but we will discuss more about this later.)

While a request for proposal (or engagement letter) is by definition an indicator that a buyer is in the Formal Buying stage, there is another indicator that may help a seller know the buyer is getting close to that stage. This indicator is the inclusion or involvement of all the key decision makers or influencers. Let me explain with a personal example.

I am a musician and my primary instrument is guitar. I greatly enjoy window shopping for guitars at various music stores. I read magazines that present information about new guitars and evaluate guitars that I have not had the opportunity to play. My beautiful wife enjoys my guitar playing; however, she really has no interest at all in going to music stores or reading guitar magazines. (I wonder why?) So, I generally do these things on my own. That said, if I were to decide to purchase a new guitar, I would not just go out and buy it without discussing it with my wife. Our family's finances are something we discuss and pray about together. We also make significant financial decisions together. So, I may indeed spend a lot of time alone window shopping and defining my wants and needs with music equipment, but I would bring my wife into the equation when I am ready to make a purchase decision.

I have observed a similar thing in business-to-business sales. Many times CFOs or other decision makers will go through the early stages of the buyer's decision process on their own. Sometimes it is simply easier to keep the number of people involved to a minimum. Other times they may not have the support yet of other key decision makers or influencers, so they keep them out of the process intentionally until later. However, once they enter into the Formal Buying stage, they must bring all relevant parties to the table. That is why, at times, new players enter into the process late in the game, often to the seller's surprise and dismay. Unfortunately, even diligent sellers cannot always prevent these surprises from occurring. However, it is helpful to know if you begin to see new players emerge, you could deduce that perhaps the buyer is getting close to the Formal Buying stage.

STAGE 4—DECISION

We are now to the final stage a buyer goes through in a purchasing decision, and that is the Decision stage itself. While much has been made over the years regarding this stage of the buying process, I tend to agree with those who state the decision is a natural outflow of each of the preceding stages. The outcome has largely been determined by the time the buyer enters this stage. I do not subscribe to the notion of "closers" brought in to secure or save the day.

While I acknowledge the negotiation and closing stage needs to be handled skillfully, I think bringing in a "closer" who hasn't been thoroughly involved in the overall sales process is a manipulative play. The exception would be a company bringing in one key executive to the closing table to demonstrate the importance of the business relationship to the selling company. Such an investment can be a highly positive gesture in the right circumstances. However, this is for relationship enhancement.

The Decision stage is the time when buyers evaluate what they have learned and assess whether the selling company will live up to its commitments. Buyers also make many soft assessments at this stage, such as an assessment of the "chemistry" between the buyer's team and the seller's team.

The most significant role a seller can play at this stage is availability and support. The team should be available to answer questions that arise and give support to the buyer by providing any additional information or scheduling any additional discussions that are needed to finalize a decision. Sellers should be proactive and regular in communications at this stage, but should balance communications so as not to be impatient or a pest. The best way to be proactive is to suggest specific times when the seller will follow up with the buyer, and then to follow through as agreed.

Unfortunately, the buying process doesn't just flow from window shopping to decision without any hindrances. Therefore we need to discuss the barriers and challenges that may arise and keep buyers stuck before they reach the Decision stage. Understanding these barriers enables sellers to help buyers move through the decision process.

BARRIERS AND CHALLENGES

While the activities in the Window Shopping and Wants/Needs Defined stages work in close concert, movement from the Wants/Needs Defined stage to the Formal Buying stage, and from the Formal Buying stage to a Decision stage requires the buyer to face and address specific barriers. Let's look at some of them next.

CLARITY

The first barrier that buyers encounter is the need to gain clarity on the specifics of their needs and the corresponding requirements needed in a solution. While this seems like an elementary observation, it is important to note that frequently it is this step that is poorly handled.

Buyers handle it poorly when they are in haste for a solution and do not take adequate time to fully examine needs or potential solutions.

Sellers (particularly inexperienced or nontraditional sellers) handle it poorly because in their excitement, discomfort, or impatience with the selling process, they focus on the first need or requirement mentioned by the potential buyer and fail to take the time to fully understand the other factors facing the buyer. In fact, it is not uncommon for them to miss the real need entirely because they become fixated either on the first issue mentioned, or worse, on some product or service they assume the buyer wants or needs.

Sellers need to ask question that allow them to understand all issues the buyer is facing—the needs behind the needs. Sellers must understand that buyers will at times talk about their easy or less-threatening challenges first rather than having to discuss those issues that may be more difficult for them.

In summary, when buyers are in the Window Shopping stage, they are working to educate themselves on the number and types of solutions available in the marketplace related to their given need. They will often enter into the Window Shopping stage with a short list of solution requirements, but it is the exercise of Window Shopping that provides them with an understanding of the options available to them and the benefits of various solution alternatives. As they learn about solution alternatives, they begin to expand or change their solution requirements (wish list) and in turn narrow down the number of potential solutions. In doing so, they also narrow the list of potential solution providers. In other words, they are gaining clarity on their situation and options, which will allow them to define and better communicate their wants and needs, both internally and externally.

CONSTRAINTS

The next barrier is constraints. A constraint by definition is a limitation or restriction. In our discussion of a purchasing decision, a constraint is something that buyers perceive will prevent or hinder them from moving forward in a purchasing decision. Generally a constraint is believed to be something that stems from present circumstances outside of the buyer's control.

For example, once a buyer has evaluated wants and needs and has developed a list of requirements in a solution, buyers must evaluate the costs of that solution against their limitations of personal or corporate resources. The most obvious limited resource is money. Simply put, does the buyer have the financial resources to afford the solution? Another limited resource is time. Does the buyer have the time to pursue or implement the solution? In a corporate setting, the time constraint is often translated as having the necessary staff or manpower to implement the solution. Another common constraint revolves around the political clout of the buyer. Do they have the authority, leadership team support, or influence to move forward with the decision?

The constraints listed here are common, but they are not the only existing limitations. The main thing to remember is that in the minds of buyers these limitations prevent them from proceeding further. Even if they want to solve their need, they can't solve it unless the limitation is removed or other alternatives present themselves. Sellers need to discuss these issues with their buyers, but please remember to be delicate in your approach. Buyers may be sensitive about their limitations (whether you are talking budget, authority, etc.).

RISKS

The third key barrier present in any major purchase decision is risk, which is subtler than the previous two barriers. It is subtle because is rests more on perceptions and concerns than it does on direct or measurable limitations.

When a purchase decision is stalled or halted due to constraints, the buyer feels like he or she can't move forward, even if there is a desire to. When a purchase decision is stalled or halted due to risk, buyers are not sure if they want to proceed. Buyers are concerned about the potential problems that could arise if they make a wrong or less-than-optimal decision. At times, they may reassess whether they really have to meet the need at all.

It is very important for the seller to explore the risks that concern their buyers. As you understand the risks your buyers are struggling with, you will gain a great amount of insight into your buyers. This insight will help you assist your buyer in making more informed decisions.

There are many areas of risk surrounding a major purchasing decision. Some risks are directly business related and some are personal. Business risks include the risk of

solving the wrong problem (opportunity cost)

choosing the wrong solution

choosing the wrong solution provider

missing the mark—deadlines, intended results, budget requirements

disrupting the balance established by previous service providers

Personal risks include the impact of the decision on:

personal work load and department work load

professional relationships (co-workers, venders, etc.)

personal relationships (referral sources, former employers)

career path (good decision—promotions, bonuses, etc.)

career path (bad decision—job stability, bonuses, etc.)

This is by no means intended to be an exhaustive list. The important thing to remember is that these risks, whether real or perceived, will have an impact on the buyer's motivations and actions. The larger the decision, the more factors will be considered.

DEALING WITH BARRIERS

Barriers are present in any sales opportunity. The strength of the barrier may vary, but most barriers can be overcome. Exploring barriers and developing approaches for dealing with them are often what occupies a seller's attention.

There are four different approaches to barriers. You can find a way to eliminate the barrier, mitigate the barrier, overcome the barrier, or agree that the barrier is indeed firm and immovable. Let's examine these four approaches.

ELIMINATE

The best way to deal with a barrier is to eliminate it. While certainly ideal, this option is not always possible. At the same time, you shouldn't dismiss the potential. Sometimes a barrier is based on a belief that can be challenged. Let's suppose for example the buyer is struggling with a concern about a purchase risk. It may be that the buyer's concern is actually unfounded because the buyer is basing the concern on incomplete information, a misunderstanding of facts, or an assumption. If the seller can provide the buyer with concrete information that displaces or combats these concerns, then the seller eliminates the barrier.

MITIGATE

Another way to deal with a barrier is to address its figurative size, weight, or height. When making a purchase decision, a buyer often can magnify the challenge by placing too much focus on the challenge so that it becomes exaggerated and overwhelming. As a seller, you can bring objectivity to the subject.

The word *mitigate* means to lessen the force or intensity and to reduce the severity of an issue or circumstance. If, as a seller, you can help a buyer mitigate the barrier, you will open the potential of the buyer being able to get past that barrier. How do you do this? There is no single answer to this question, but I can give you some examples and suggestions.

One way to mitigate a barrier is to address it objectively. If indeed the buyer has exaggerated the severity of the circumstance, at times a discussion addressing the challenge head on can help. The seller can help the buyer get a handle on the weight of the issue, and in turn, can offer suggestions for dealing with it. Another way to mitigate a barrier is to offer a way in which you as a seller can help lessen the impact of the issue.

For example, I was once pursuing a large state and local tax engagement with a major manufacturer. The key decision maker I was working with told our team that she was concerned about the effect of moving forward with the engagement on interdepartmental relations with the accounts payable department. Apparently relationships were somewhat strained and this tax director, while focused first on what was best for the company, was still struggling with the effect of the decision. The way we chose to mitigate her concern was simply to back up the sales process and have another meeting with the company where both departments were represented. By doing this, the burden of building the business case to the A/P department shifted to us and not on the tax director. We were able to move past this particular barrier by mitigating its impact.

OVERCOME

The next approach to dealing with a barrier is more assertive. It comes by placing an emphasis on the strength of the solution the seller suggests to the buyer. This approach is comparing the risk to the reward. This can be a powerful approach, and it is particularly effective when dealing with financial barriers.

For example, let's suppose you work for a firm that provides health care consulting services, specifically assisting hospitals to identify problems in their handling of Medicare reimbursements. You assist hospitals in understanding and accurately applying the Medicare rules to help ensure they are receiving the appropriate level of payment for the services they provide. It may not surprise you that many hospitals don't have a large budget for consulting services. And yet, if you as a seller can describe the revenue potential available to the hospital if they engaged your service and can demonstrate by past example how your clients generally received a strong multiple in return for the fees invested, then you can likely overcome the financial barrier and potentially win the engagement.

AGREE

The fourth option is to agree. There **are** barriers that are too big, risky, or challenging to tackle at a particular moment in time. After reviewing the buyer's circumstances and evaluating alternatives for dealing with the constraints or risks the individual or company faces, you may come to the conclusion that moving forward is not the wisest course of action for the buyer at this time. This option must always be on the table if a seller wants to maintain integrity. Remember the seller's role is to help a buyer make a wise, well informed buying decision. Sometimes this means the best answer for the prospect is not to move forward with a purchase decision.

ADDITIONAL CONSIDERATIONS—BREAKING DOWN BARRIERS

Sometimes a barrier presented in a sales situation may appear to be a "deal breaker." In these situations it is important to consider the makeup of the barrier itself. Sometimes you may determine, as previously stated, that the barrier is too great, and it is not in the best interest of the buyer to move forward. However, some barriers can be broken down into smaller subconcerns and you may be able to address those individually. If you can address many of the subconcerns, you may be able to address the global barrier sufficiently.

For example, let's suppose you are pursuing work with a plastics injection molding manufacturer, and the prospect states that he will only engage a firm that has experience working with plastics injection molding companies. Let's further suppose your firm does not have that direct experience. What do you do? Will it work to simply continue "building the relationship"? I would say, probably not.

When presented with such a challenge, it appears that we are shut out. After all, if the buyer simply asks the question, "Do you have experience with plastics injection molding companies?" your answer will be no. Therefore, it appears as though you will need to give up.

For the buyer's best interest, you must first confirm that you have the capabilities to effectively serve them. If you do not, you should professionally back out of the pursuit. However, let's say that your firm has strong experience with manufacturers, just not with plastics injection molding manufacturers. Yes, there are distinctions between segments, but the core work, and most of the specialized needs that manufacturers have are similar, and you are well versed in those areas.

I would then contend that you shouldn't give up yet. You may still have a chance of success. In the example, it appears that your firm has been placed in a binary (yes or no) situation. This is a time to "break down" the barrier.

Generally, an objection such as this rests on the buyer's concern about risk. Therefore, we need to further explore those risks with the buyer. My suggestion would be to request an opportunity to meet once again with the buyer and hold a discussion similar to this example:

Mr. Smith, when we spoke the other day you mentioned you would not hire a firm unless it had experience with plastics injection molding companies, is that right?

[**Mr.** Smith confirms.]

I wanted to confirm this is so that I could understand your concerns. You need to know that presently our firm does not have direct experience with plastics injection molding companies, so it would appear we don't meet your criteria. We wanted to explore this a bit more if we could.

We do have significant experience with other process manufacturers, such as metal stamping, flat rolled steel, textile, and machinery manufacturers. Each of these businesses is different, but we have found that their needs are quite similar.

Would you elaborate on some specific areas of concern? In other words, would you mind sharing the risks you see in hiring a firm who hasn't worked in your industry?

To which areas do you see a firm with direct experience adding additional value?

[**Facilitate** a discussion where concerns are specified. Take detailed notes.]

We appreciate your time. To confirm I have heard you correctly, your key concerns are: [review concise structured list of concerns]

With your permission we would like to review these concerns as a team and come back with specific approaches to address them, and ideas where we may be able to add value. Could we set up another time to talk?

In this example, the seller is working to take the single concern (Do you have experience in my industry?) and replace that concern with a list of specific concerns. The benefit to buyers is that they will gain a more specific picture of their needs as they work to articulate the concerns. The advantage to sellers is that they are no longer working against a binary (yes/no) concern. In most cases, the seller will actually be able to address a number (if not most) of the articulated concerns, thus substantiating their position and increasing their chance of success.

Now that we have reviewed the four stages a buyer goes through in making a major decision and have examined the barriers or obstacles that may be faced, let's assemble the full Buyer's Decision Model. This model attempts to portray the interrelation of both the stages and the barriers in a way that describes the progression of a decision.

BUILDING THE BUYER'S DECISION MODEL

The Buyer's Decision Model is the most important model presented in this book, so I would ask you to pay close attention to this section as we build the model piece by piece. Once fully developed, the Buyer's Decision Model (Figure 5.2) will become the foundation for determining what Next Steps must be taken to move a buyer toward a decision and, hopefully, a favorable one.

One of the interrelations depicted in the Buyer's Decision Model is the order of the elements. While this interrelation should be self-explanatory, it is this very order of elements that can confuse nontraditional sellers and, at times, experienced sellers. The reason for this confusion is the unique chain of events that takes place in each sales pursuit. You can be reasonably assured no two sales opportunities appear alike on the surface. If you stay at the surface or activity level, there are no formulas to be applied universally. However, the lack of consistency on the surface can be deceiving. In each purchase decision, regardless of the order or nature of events on the surface, the core of the purchase decision actually does remain the same.

Buyers do not make a decision without first knowing what they want and need for themselves or their company/firm. Generally a buyer doesn't have a clear idea of what he or she wants or needs, unless he or she has been made aware of alternative solutions. The time and importance placed on each stage differs from buyer to buyer and sale to sale, but they occur, and generally in the order shown in Figure 5.2.

As for the barriers, there are some distinctions to consider. Each of the barriers mentioned earlier are evaluated and faced in every purchase decision; however, the order of discussion and exploration can vary greatly, depending on the buyer's personality, authority, history, and risk tolerance. It is not unusual for the buyer to begin examining risks and constraints early in the buying process, only to reexamine them again prior to making a decision. So, don't let the order of elements throw you. Treat the exploration and management of barriers as milestones that must be achieved during each sale, rather than as a numeric "step" in a sales process.

I have frequently been challenged regarding the importance of bringing up risks and constraints if the buyer has not brought up specific issues. The concern primarily rests on a fear that any discussion of a perceived weakness will hurt our opportunity for the sale. While on the surface this makes sense, a closer examination may lead you to a different conclusion. If a buyer has a concern related to a risk or constraint, then the individual has the concern. Just because the buyer hasn't vocalized concerns doesn't remove the barrier.

Let's suppose a buyer's concern has the potential of shifting the likelihood of the sale to your competitor. Let's depict this decision as a seesaw. In Figure 5.3, the

FIGURE 5.2 **THE BUYER'S DECISION MODEL**

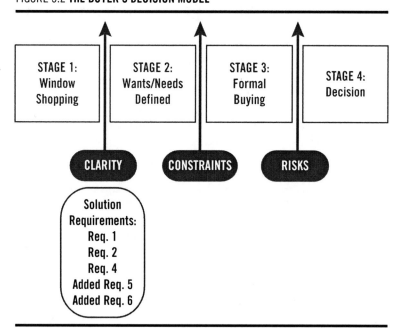

- 58 -

buyer believes going with your competitor is a less risky decision. The balance falls in favor of your competitor. The question at hand is—what will shift the balance in your favor?

Before answering that question, I have another question for you. If the buyer is leaning toward going with the competitor because he or she feels there is less risk, how does it benefit the seller not to discuss that buyer's area of concern? Is it likely that the buyer's mind will change without a new perspective or further evidence?

Sellers can employ one of three tactics to shift the balance of the equation in their favor:

1. They can add weight to their business case by taking actions to reduce the buyer's real or perceived risk.

2. They can attempt to weaken the business case of the competitor. (This author does not support downplaying or talking negatively about the competition.)

3. They can shift the balance of the equation by shifting the pivot (focal) point.

Items 1 provides the buyer with better information, allowing the buyer to reevaluate options. This author avoids item 2. Item 3 can actually be a stronger option, when it's handled appropriately. In this situation, the seller redirects the focus of the buyer to the importance of other selling points, which are actually of equal or greater importance.

This third example may be harder to follow, so let's look at it like this. Suppose you are selling audit services to a company whose management thinks they need to use a "Big 4" audit firm. You are not a "Big 4" firm. How might the third point from this list apply? It may be as simple as this.

"Mr. CFO, I know that in the past your company has only used 'Big 4' firms to perform your audit, and your main reason for that was your intent to take your

FIGURE 5.3 **YOU VS. THEM**

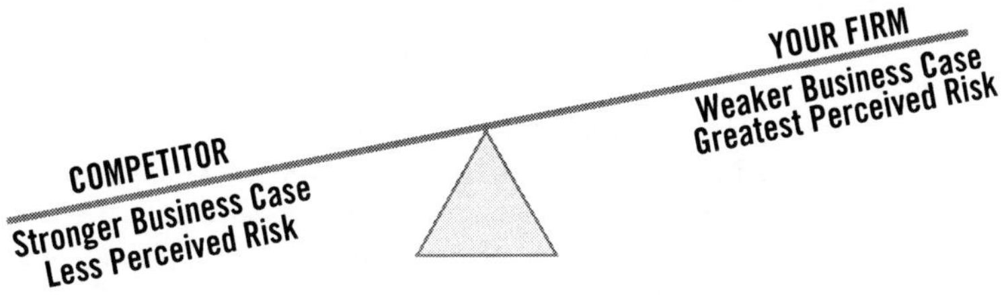

company public. Based on our discussions, I understand that you now intend to stay a private company, and the IPO is off the table. With this being the case, do you still feel that you need to pay the fee premium of retaining a 'Big 4' firm, or do you feel a smaller firm may be able to serve your needs now?"

In this example, the plan to take the company public acts as the pivot (decision) point of the seesaw. If indeed this point is no longer relevant, then the entire pivot point of the decision can be shifted, and with it the balance of weight. Such a shift could work to the seller's advantage.

To follow through on any of these techniques, you must address issues head-on, discussing them openly and fully with your buyer. You must understand what the concerns are behind the concerns. You also must understand what the most important things to the buyer are. Only then can you work to best meet the buyer's needs.

I emphasize again, the most important thing in this process is for the buyer to find the best solution. Sometimes that is your solution. Other times, it is actually your competitor's solution. The techniques given here and throughout the book are intended to direct your attention to activities that can help both you and your buyer come to the best solution.

BUYER'S DECISION MODEL—ADDITIONAL CONSIDERATIONS

The purpose of any model is to provide structure, or a framework, from which to work. Next, we will outline a method that will help sellers quickly determine an effective next step as they work with buyers in the decision process. However, before we review this method, some additional items should be considered.

First, no model will fully address every situation that can occur during a complex sale. Using a model will help put structure to your pursuit, will help you with your pursuit strategy, and will help you effectively determine next steps. However, no model can substitute for listening, introspection, and careful thought when buyers throw curve balls your way. Hopefully with a good understanding of the Buyer's Decision Model, you will understand and anticipate more, and therefore, fewer situations will become curve balls for you as the seller.

Second, in most complex selling situations, there are a number of parties involved. Some are decision makers; some are decision influencers. These additional parties can be part of the organization, related parties, or individuals outside the organization. Inside the organization, you will find key company executives, departmental leaders, and interested internal parties who will be directly affected by the purchasing decision. Related parties include investors and board members, as well as the key executives from parent companies who have influence over the purchasing decision. Outside the organization will be those individuals who can influence the buyer due to their personal and professional credibility.

As you prepare to use the Buyer's Decision Model, the first question you will need to answer is "Who are the key people involved in the decision?" This will include the decision maker and the top decision influencers. Why is this important? If multiple parties are significantly involved, then you may have a Buyer's Decision Model for each party. As you examine where each of these key decision makers and influencers are in their model, and how they interrelate, you will gain a fresh perspective on the pursuit, and often develop more creative approaches. Just don't overdo it. Keep things as simple as you can. Only examine a model for each party that will significantly affect the decision.

As an example, let us suppose you are selling to the CFO of a large subsidiary of an international corporation. Let us further suppose that the international parent company needs to be consulted or will weigh-in on the purchase decision.

To determine Next Steps, we would want to consider where key buyers are in their decision process. To do so, we would consider a Buyer's Decision Model for each key decision maker. In our example, the seller would chart two Buyer's Decision Models—one for the CFO and one for the key decision maker at the parent company. Chapter 6 describes this process.

CHAPTER
SIX

DETERMINING NEXT STEPS WITH CASE STUDIES

s you just learned, one of the main insights you gain by using the Buyer's Decision Model comes from recognizing that while there is one decision to be made, each **decision maker** will be at different stages, and facing different barriers, throughout the decision process. These differences add complexity to the sale and frequently are the reason for unexpected twists during a pursuit. Surprises come about when a seller is too focused on a single decision maker/influencer, and not recognizing or supporting the needs of each key party.

Using a Buyer's Decision Model for each key decision maker allows us to map out the decision process. This map can be used by the seller to guide each decision maker through his or her discovery of needs, examination of options (window shopping), definition of needs (solution criteria), into their formal decision process, and on to the decision.

THE PROCESS OF DETERMINING NEXT STEPS ▬▬

For the sake of instruction, the following process is given in a mechanical way, to help the reader use the model to the fullest benefit. Over time, mechanics will give way to understanding and most of the process of determining Next Steps will be done quickly in your head or through discussion. I encourage you to follow the mechanical steps until the thought process becomes fully understood and ingrained.

Determining Next Steps includes:

- **S:** Survey the situation
- **T:** Target the barriers
- **E:** Examine objectives
- **P:** Prioritize your next steps

SURVEY THE SITUATION (S)

You may not know where each decision maker is and may determine that one is not even in the model yet. They could be currently satisfied with the status quo. Assessing where each decision maker and influencer is will influence your determination of Next Steps. The following lists what you need to do to survey the situation:

1. Identify key decision makers and influencers.
2. Assess interpersonal dynamics that could affect the decision. This includes the influence of family dynamics, existing relationships, investors, advisors, and so on.
3. Identify competition.
4. Assess competitive dynamics (relationships, reputation, expertise, and risks).
5. Draw a simplified Buyer's Decision Model for each key decision maker and influencer.
6. Assess where each decision maker/influencer is in his or her decision process and mark the model.

TARGET THE BARRIERS (T)

After surveying the situation (S), consider what barriers exist to each buyer or decision maker choosing your solution. Follow these steps to target those barriers (T):

1. Identify barriers each decision maker/influencer is facing (clarity, constraints, risks). *What is keeping each from advancing toward a decision?*
2. Write down the key barriers. Be as specific as possible. For example, "The project's impact on departmental workload due to staffing constraints and high turnover."
3. If you are unsure of the barrier a buyer is facing, your next step defaults to investigation:

   - **Solution criteria:** Does the buyer have a clear picture of a good solution?
   - **Constraints:** Do we know which constraints the buyer is facing?
   - **Risks:** Do we fully understand all the concerns of the buyer?

EXAMINE OBJECTIVES (E)

Using the Next Steps approach allows you to look ahead, enabling you to gain clarity on several objectives for each decision maker (i.e., a series of next steps). This is a benefit of the Next Steps approach—you begin to see a path to success, rather than just your next move. Follow these steps to examine objectives (E):

1. Review known variables:

   - Interpersonal dynamics
   - Competitive dynamics

- The stage each decision maker/influencer is in
- The barriers each decision maker/influencer is facing

2. Determine objectives. Objectives will generally be:
   - To reengage communication when channels have closed
   - To gain an introduction to another decision maker/influencer
   - To further explore specific information (solution criteria, constraints, or risks)
   - To specifically address a barrier (eliminate, mitigate, overcome, or agree)

PRIORITIZE NEXT STEPS (P)

Finally, you should prioritize your Next Steps (P) by taking these steps:

1. Prioritize.
2. Assign tasks (objectives).
3. Set a timetable for each task.
4. Take action.

It will initially take time to determine your next steps. However, as the concepts become ingrained, you will find that the entire STEP process only takes minutes. You will know what your prospect needs, what you will do to meet those needs, and why.

Additionally, as you use the model consistently, you will naturally begin to incorporate it into your inquiry and thought processes. This will impact your approach to prospects and toward each sale. This, in turn, will increase your efficiency and effectiveness.

ADDITIONAL SALES GUIDANCE

EVERYTHING RESTS ON COMMUNICATION

Nothing productive happens if there is no communication. When I say nothing productive, I am referring to the advancement of the sale. Communication is essential for every step of the process. Yes, the seller can do things such as research and preparation, but none of these things (in themselves) have an impact on the sale. If you are pursuing a buyer and communication has stopped, or been hindered, then restoration of a channel of communication is your primary charge. **It must be your next step.**

DON'T GO IT ALONE

Another important consideration in any sales pursuit is the makeup of the sales team. Up to this point, I have referred to the seller as an individual. However, in most complex sales situations, you are selling as a team to a team. And in most cases this is preferable. Having a sales team gives you the potential advantage of complimentary skills. You can play off of each other's strengths and better match personalities. You also demonstrate to buyers that they are receiving the strength and backing of a company, rather than just an individual. This gives buyers greater assurance. So, if you are indeed pursuing an opportunity alone, and have the opportunity of developing a sales team, I recommend doing so.

DON'T SKIP STEPS

As a seller, you should discipline yourself so as not to rush the buyer through the decision process. Each of the stages a buyer goes through is present for a reason. Even the barriers serve a good purpose for the buyer—and yes—even for the seller.

You may enter a selling situation any place along the buyer's decision process. As a seller, it is vitally important that you work with your buyer on all stages of the decision. A buyer may have already gone through each stage, and barrier, and done so carefully. However, some buyers may not have examined all issues as diligently as they should.

If you find yourself thinking, "So what," I would challenge you to examine your motives and make sure you are working to serve your buyer's interest first. The "so what" is simply this, if buyers have not carefully gone through all the stages of the decision process, they may not:

- Be aware of all the options
- Have clearly defined their needs and wants
- Have carefully weighed their needs and wants against their resources
- Have carefully weighed their needs and wants against their risks
- End up with the best solution

This should be very important to you as a seller.

You need to be aware that even if a buyer has been diligent in the purchasing process prior to your arrival, you are handicapped because you don't know what the individual or company has evaluated. You don't know why the buyer has arrived at his or her current conclusions.

When you come into the buyer's decision late in the process, you may have a competitor who has walked through the earlier stages with the buyer. This means your competitor has an advantage over you. As a seller, you need to go back to the beginning with the buyer and make sure you have covered all the bases. This does not need to be a long, drawn-out process. It could potentially be handled in one conversation, but don't omit, gloss over, or rush this step. Remember, one of your biggest competitive advantages is to understand your buyer's needs, wants, and concerns better than your competition. If you can identify additional solution requirements the buyer may have, you will likely be the only competitor to include those requirements in your solution offering, and the buyer will feel that he or she has a true resource.

PRACTICE CASE STUDIES

Let's now put the Next Steps approach to use with a few case studies.

CASE STUDY 1

BACKGROUND

You just received a request for proposal (RFP) to perform auditing for Smith College, a small private college in rural North Carolina. You haven't heard of Smith College before and are not sure how they heard of your firm or got your name. The RFP arrived with plenty of time and is not due for 5 weeks. You research Smith's website thoroughly. You decide to call Chuck Bolan, a college friend of yours who is a CPA at a firm in North Carolina. Chuck works primarily on governmental clients, but does audit one private college. Chuck says Smith College is only about 18 years old and has used the same small CPA firm since it formed. He also said that they have considerable endowments. He then laughs and lets you know that he received the RFP too. You place a call to Jane Newman (the CFO of Smith College) to discuss the opportunity and gain more background. Jane doesn't answer, but her assistant Todd Aarons takes the call. Todd explains that Jane is in meetings for the remainder of the week, and that she will be out the following two weeks: one week on vacation, and the other to attend the Southern Association of College and University Business Officers (SACUBO) conference and some SACUBO committee meetings.

CHALLENGE

What do you do now? What should be your next steps? Why?

RESPONSE

1. Survey the Situation (S)

At the present time the only decision maker you know is the CFO, Jane Newman. You know that Jane is in the formal buying stage because Smith College has issued an RFP. Asking for bids in writing (by definition) falls under the Formal Buying stage (as shown in Figure 6.1).

You can summarize the rest of the situation as:

- Interpersonal dynamics: Unknown
- **Competitive dynamics:** Unknown
- **Key decision maker:** Jane Newman, CFO
- Other decision makers/influencers: Unknown

2. Target the Barriers (T)

Other than specific concerns that may be raised within the RFP, the barriers that Jane Newman and Smith College are facing are unknown to you at this time.

3. Examine Objectives (E)

Based on the current situation you have several objectives:

- Gain an introductory meeting with Jane Newman, CFO.
- Identify other key decision makers.
- Work to identify any interpersonal dynamics that could impact the decision.
- Identify the competition and assess their strengths and weaknesses.
- Develop an understanding of the solution criteria **beyond those** listed in the RFP.
- Explore the constraints the college is facing.
- Explore the risks the college is facing in this decision.
- Complete the following exploration with within the next 3 weeks to allow time for proposal production and delivery.

FIGURE 6.1 **JANE NEWMAN'S STAGE**

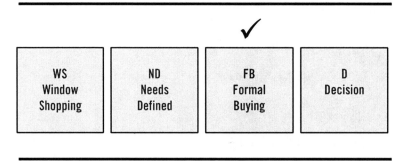

4. Prioritize Next Steps (P)

The first priority among the objectives listed in step 3 is to secure a communication channel through an introductory meeting with Jane Newman. Your goal is to gain understanding on each of the objectives you've listed. This is a challenging position to be in. The timetable of the RFP, in conjunction with Jane's availability over the next 2 to 3 weeks may make the opportunity futile, unless:

- You can secure a meeting with Jane prior to her vacation.
- Jane provides you with the names of other key decision makers on this pursuit who have clear insight into the challenges.
- You can communicate the importance to Smith College of detailed discussion and negotiate an extension of the RFP deadline.

While it may appear this case study represents a strong sales opportunity (since the buyer is in the formal buying stage), it actually illustrates the poor position a firm is in when responding to unsolicited RFPs. This is particularly the case when no previous communication or relationships exist. In these situations, the seller must gain an understanding of many factors in a very condensed time frame to gain any level of competitive strength.

CASE STUDY 2

BACKGROUND

You have an opportunity to pursue Parker Construction, a large construction company with $80 million in annual revenue. The company is a second-generation family owned business. Parker's president is 52-year-old Bill Parker, the son of William Parker Senior. William is 76 years old and officially retired; nevertheless, he has remained actively involved with the company. William comes to the office a couple of days a week to help the company negotiate and sell new projects. He is also present for every executive meeting and has a considerable influence on Bill. Parker Construction has done quite well despite the economy due to the types of construction projects they engage in, principally heavy highway construction. Because of William's influence, Parker Construction operates with little debt and is cash rich. Bill thinks the time is right to take a big step and acquire a couple of local construction companies. Both of these companies focus on different niches than Parker Construction today. This diversification is part of the appeal for Bill. If these acquisitions take place, the company would add about $35 million to its annual revenue, in addition to more complexity.

Currently, a small, 2-partner local firm serves Parker Construction. The partner on the account is a personal friend of William's, and is 71 years old. Bill thinks it is important to secure a firm that can help them move the company forward, but he knows his father will want them to stay with the existing firm, even if it means switching to their new junior (56-year-old) partner. He is concerned about his father's position.

CHALLENGE

Bill has hired you to conduct some due diligence on one of the potential acquisition candidates. You really want the opportunity to secure Parker Construction as a full-service client. How do you deal with the dynamics between Bill and William? What are your next steps? Why?

RESPONSE

1. Survey the Situation (S)

In this study, there are two models (Figure 6.2): one for Bill as the decision maker, and one for William as a key decision influencer. Bill has made a decision to use your firm for a due diligence project, but he is in the window shopping stage as it relates to the entirety of their work. William is not even on the decision model. He is in "status quo" mode and not looking to change.

FIGURE 6.2 **TWO BUYER'S STAGES**

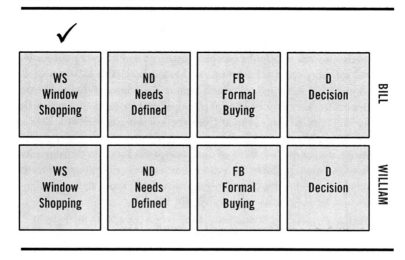

Your survey has uncovered the following:

- Interpersonal dynamics:
  - William's influence over Bill
  - William's relationship with the lead partner of their existing firm
- Competitive dynamics:

  - Existing firm is solidly entrenched
  - Existing firm's lead partner will likely transition soon
  - Your firm has been hired to do some advisory work

2. Target the Barriers (T)

Barriers impacting Bill currently include the risk associated with his father's response to Bill's consideration of changing firms and the necessity to establish clarity on his needs. Since William is not in the decision model, he is not currently facing any barriers.

3. Examine Objectives (E)

You are able to identify a handful of known objectives at this time:

- Help Bill gain clarity on his needs, and therefore build his solution criteria.
- Utilize the Four Catalysts to shift William toward the Window Shopping stage.

4. Prioritize Next Steps (P)

The key barrier facing Bill right now appears to be the risk associated with suggesting a change to his father. However, the Buyer's Decision Model helps you understand that addressing this risk is premature, because its importance rests closer to the decision stage. Since Bill is currently in the Window Shopping stage his pressing barrier is to establish clarity on his needs (the solution criteria).

Yes, Bill knows what his company's needs have been in the past, however should Parker Construction move forward with the potential mergers, the company's needs will change and become more complex. Therefore Bill needs assistance defining and gaining clarity on these needs. An understanding of these needs will also assist Bill later when he approaches his father to discuss changing firms. He may be able to demonstrate that their existing firm cannot meet all their requirements. So your priority Next Step is to set up a meeting with Bill to clarify his needs and build his solution criteria.

SIMPLIFYING COMPLEX SALES

CASE STUDY 3

BACKGROUND

A little over a year ago your firm submitted a proposal on the audit of Robinson Manufacturing, a subsidiary of AXIS Manufacturing, a large, privately held company based in New Jersey. Two global firms (one the incumbent), one national firm, and another large regional firm competed against your firm for the opportunity. Although your firm had no prior relationship with Robinson or AXIS, you felt you had built good rapport with Robinson's management team, in particular with the CFO, Max. During the pursuit, Max explained that their reason for going out to bid was poor service from their current firm.

Based on discussions with Max, you understood that the same firm currently audited AXIS and Robinson but that Robinson could make a decision on their audit autonomously from AXIS. They expressed an interest in switching from a global firm and communicated that your firm was one of two they were favoring. The decision process extended several weeks past the date originally given. Once contacted, you were surprised to discover that Robinson had elected to retain their existing firm. You requested a follow-up discussion and were told by Max that AXIS had overruled Robinson's recommendation based on new service-level commitments that the global firm had provided in their rebid process. Though you tried asking twice, Max wouldn't say whether your firm was their recommended choice.

CURRENT

Last weekend you went to a social event and ran into Max. During your conversation, you asked him how things were going with their current firm. Twenty minutes later Max ceased his rant. He was obviously very disappointed with the service they were receiving. He stated that they got almost no time from their engagement partner, and that most calls take two or three days to be returned. Additionally, they just found out that the current audit firm was going to change the manager on their account for the upcoming audit year. Due to the social setting and other people joining the conversation, the focus shifted and Max was now deep into a discussion about a recent football game. After some time, you excused yourself and got back into the swing of the party.

CHALLENGE

It is now Monday; you are back in your office, remembering your conversation with Max on Saturday night. You are trying to assess whether there is an opportunity or not, and if so, what you should do about it. What do you do?

1. Survey the Situation (S)

Your survey has uncovered the following:

- **Interpersonal dynamics:**
  - Relationship between AXIS and Robinson Manufacturing
  - Your relationship and the confidence your team has earned with Robinson Manufacturing

- **Competitive dynamics:**
  - Max's dissatisfaction with his current audit firm
  - AXIS management's previous service-level commitment concerns
  - AXIS management's current level of satisfaction is unknown
  - Your knowledge of which firms were involved in the previous RFP process

- **Decision makers/influencers:**
  - Max at Robinson Manufacturing
  - Management at AXIS

In this case, the primary interpersonal dynamics are the relationship between the parent company (AXIS) and Robinson Manufacturing. While management from Robinson have asserted their autonomy on certain decisions, we know now from experience that their decisions can be vetoed by their parent company. Therefore, any opportunity with Robinson will require approval from AXIS.

Another dynamic involves the relationship you've built and confidence earned between Max and your team during the previous proposal process. These dynamics may provide you with leverage in future discussions.

At this time you know that Max, the CFO, is frustrated with the service he is receiving from his existing firm. You also know that at least a year ago, the parent company had some concerns resulting in new service-level commitments from the global firm. You do not know whether the parent company is currently satisfied or dissatisfied with the service they are receiving for the overall organization.

Additionally, you know which firms were involved with the bid last year. You do not know if any of these firms have remained in active communication with Robinson. After all it was only by happenstance that you became aware of Max's dissatisfaction.

There are two primary decision makers—Max at Robinson and management at AXIS. Although, you do not know who within AXIS was (and is) involved in any decision process related to their CPA firm relationship.

What you know currently is that Max is very dissatisfied, and that he can articulate specific reasons for his dissatisfaction. Based on this information you can assess that Max has specific requirements in his mind related to client service and that his existing firm is not meeting those requirements. Therefore, you should place Max in the Needs Defined stage (Figure 6.3), at least in terms of his

FIGURE 6.3 **STAGE IN DECISION PROCESS**

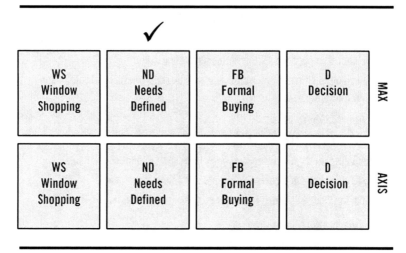

motivation. In other words, if the decision were solely up to Max, he would likely be engaged in the process of evaluating a change in providers.

AXIS at this point is a mystery. They may also be experiencing poor service and could be considering a purchase decision. They may be receiving good service (as the parent company) and unaware that the service levels within their subsidiaries is suffering. They may also be aware of the service deficiencies (if Max has been communicative.) Whether the current situation has been raised to the level of considering a RFP process is simply unknown.

2. Target the Barriers (T)

Presently the barriers that you are aware of include:

- Max's constraints on purchasing authority at Robinson
- Potential time constraints on the existing firm to meet defined service standards

3. Examine Objectives (E)

Your objectives are to:

- Develop a comprehensive understanding of Robinson's needs (solution criteria).
- Gain an understanding of where the current provider is not meeting the solution criteria.
- Identify the key decision makers within AXIS.
- Find out where AXIS management is in term of:
  - Their satisfaction with the current provider

- Their awareness of service deficiencies at Robinson Manufacturing
- Their consideration of another purchase decision (RFP)

4. Prioritize Next Steps (P)

Based on your relationship with Max, and the information he volunteered at the party, you feel that Max is your primary communication channel. While you can likely get Max to discuss his needs further, you do not want to further frustrate him or waste your partners' time if there is no opportunity to chase. Therefore, your first priority will be to approach Max to discuss, in depth, the management structure of AXIS and his knowledge surrounding their current satisfaction of service. Your goal is to "team" with Max to see if you can move AXIS into the Buyer's Decision Model or to coach you if AXIS is already considering a provider search.

CASE STUDY 4

BACKGROUND

You are in the middle of an introductory meeting with Mike Johnson, CFO of Adventure Pizza. Adventure Pizza is a 3-year-old restaurant with two stores, which are based around a theme of outdoor adventure. The restaurants are very large in size. They contain a dining area in an all-you-can-eat buffet format. They have two good-sized rooms with large screen TVs that feature extreme sports, adventure-themed movies, and survival shows. They have one large "party" room that, when not used for parties, has nightly 30-minute "shows" spanning the spectrum from acrobatics to juggling, to educational sessions like bicycle maintenance or how-tos, and strategy around paintball games. One other room off the restaurant area houses video games, pool tables, air hockey, and the like. Leaving the restaurant area, you enter an "Extreme Adventure Park"—a double gymnasium-sized area that includes a half-court basketball play area, a ropes course, and two constantly changing obstacle courses. On the far end is "Adventure Island" that includes a treehouse, a downsized obstacle course, and some carnival-like games, and a child care area for kids under 4. Adventure Pizza is located in a mid-market town, and it has been wildly successful. In fact it is so successful that a second store was opened six months ago in a town about 3 hours away. Indications are that this location may perform even better than the original store. Mike was part of Adventure Pizza from the beginning, the primary owners Larry and Charlotte Smith were college buddies of his, and he has been given a significant equity share in the company (roughly 20%).

SITUATION

During your meeting, you discover that Larry and Charlotte Smith have decided to franchise Adventure Pizza. And they want to move forward with this aggressively.

The good news—they have decided to select a new accounting firm to assist them with this plan. The bad news (you discover)—they have already received proposals from two global firms and another large regional firm. You also learn that they had planned to make their decision next week. Mike said he had decided to meet with us because of our timing. You additionally learn that Mike had worked at one of the competing firms for 2 years right out of college. He told you that he is impressed with the team that firm has put together. He said that you could also bid on the work if you would like to.

CHALLENGE

Should you chase this opportunity? If so, what should your next steps be? How can you approach this opportunity in a way that can give you a strong chance of success?

RESPONSE

1. Survey the Situation (S)

Your survey has uncovered the following:

- Interpersonal dynamics:
  - Marriage relationship between the principal owners—Larry and Charlotte Smith
  - CFO, Mike Johnson's alumni relationship with one of the competing firms
- **Competitive dynamics:**
  - Three competing firms
  - Strong reputation of the two global firms
  - Competing firms have had sufficient time to further develop needs
  - Competing firms have had the opportunity to meet with the Smiths
- **Key decision makers/influencer:**
  - Larry and Charlotte Smith
  - Mike Johnson, CFO
- Stage of buyer's decision process:

  - Formal Buying (Bid proposals have been requested)

2. Target the Barriers (T)

Presently you are ignorant of all three barriers. Outside of core, standard service expectations for audit and tax work, you do not know the Smith's decision criteria or additional service expectations. Nor have you been able to explore the constraints and risks that the Smiths and Mike Johnson are concerned about.

The timing of the bid process requires that you target all three barriers immediately, if you are to discover a competitive advantage to win the account.

3. Examine Objectives (E)

You are able to identify a handful of known objectives at this time:

- Quickly gain an audience with Larry and Charlotte Smith
- Gain all pertinent pursuit information in one meeting
- Find a way to develop "borrowed trust" (since we don't have time to build it)

4. Prioritize Next Steps (P)

Despite time constraints, your firm thinks this company could be a key strategic client, and you decide to pursue—acknowledging your weakened sales position. The challenge that sits before you, therefore, is to accomplish all of your objectives at the same time. You plan your strategy.

Due to the time constraints you know that you do not have an opportunity to build relationships and trust over time. So, your leverage must rest on your expertise, professionalism, and sales approach. Your aim is to demonstrate your client service approach and expertise through your sales approach. To accomplish this you decide to conduct a "planning session" with the Smiths and Mike Johnson. The planning session will focus on the Four Pillars (mission, vision, strategies, and tactics) with a goal of establishing trust as a firm that can help bring their vision to reality. You will request Mike's assistance in scheduling this session later this week.

The planning session will be conducted as you would a paid consulting engagement. Therefore you will be approaching the issues almost in a third-party objective way. Your aim is to help Mike and the Smiths gain confidence due to "discoveries" they make during the session. You will bring a multidisciplinary team to the meeting, covering the core bases of accounting/auditing, tax, personal financial planning, and wealth management. This team's job during the exploratory stage of the meeting is to listen, and draft a potential "action plan." The exploratory stage of the meeting will last 60 to 90 minutes and then break for lunch.

During lunch, your team will meet and compare notes, developing a suggested action plan to present to the Smiths. Following lunch, you will meet, review the action plan, and gain feedback and prioritization. At the close of the meeting, you will provide the Smiths and Mike Johnson with two strong references and ask them to contact those references (with the objective of building "borrowed trust.")

You will then strive to submit the proposal by the first of next week.

Your plan rests on the strength of your ability to define the needs, constraints, and risks the Smiths will be facing—in a more thorough and compelling manner than our competition. If you are able to place items (even concerns) on the table that the Smiths or Mike had not considered, you may be able to demonstrate a level of expertise and professionalism that can tilt the decision in your favor.

APPLYING NEXT STEPS DAILY

The case studies we have just explored demonstrate the fact that no two sales opportunities are alike. But they also demonstrate that there are key factors that remain constant. There is a path we can follow. If we approach each opportunity with an understanding of who our buyers are and where they are in their decision process, we can develop strong Next Steps that we can use to help our buyers advance in their decision.

In summary, the Next Step process includes:

- **S:** Survey the situation.
- **T:** Target the barriers.
- **E:** Examine objectives.
- **P:** Prioritize the next steps.

And, to do this effectively, you must know:

- The interpersonal dynamics tied to the decision
- The competitive dynamics tied to the decision
- The buyer's solution criteria
- The buyer's constraints
- The buyer's risks

With all of this information, you can effectively navigate a pursuit, and you can effectively manage your sales efforts—which is the topic of the next section.

SECTION THREE

Sales Management Basics

Sales management is the discipline of helping your company achieve its growth goals by holding your sales team accountable to performance standards. However, if a sales manager simply focuses on this one thing, he or she will miss the mark.

Good sales managers genuinely care about each member of their team, as individuals, not just as profit centers. Good managers work to provide each member with the training, tools, and guidance they need to be successful. Organizationally this means they will work to help each team member operate strategically, effectively, and efficiently.

Individually this means providing service by helping each team member develop goals important to them, and then working to help them meet these personal performance goals.

Good sales management also means helping members of the sales team deal with their daily challenges by offering support and encouragement, a sounding board, or assistance in developing a specific work plan that will guide them away from unproductive activities and toward productive ones. At times this may also mean telling them the hard truth to jolt them into awareness and action. Remember, people often have blind spots when it comes to their own performance. However, for all these things to be effective and helpful, all must be motivated by genuine concern for the individual.

This section briefly reviews some of the issues you face when managing growth and supporting a sales team.

CHAPTER
SEVEN

SALES TEAM SUPPORT AND MANAGEMENT

SALES REPRESENTATIVES AS INDIVIDUALS ■■■■■

The most challenging aspect of sales management is the fact that each sales representative is different. These differences range from personality and style; to preferences and approach; to knowledge, skills, and experience. Each difference needs to be recognized and compensated for in your approach to managing their efforts.

DEALING WITH DIFFERENCES

Some people believe sales representatives must have a specific personality type: outgoing, extroverted, persuasive, competitive, and so on. This is simply not true. While I acknowledge some of these traits are helpful in sales, the truth is that there is not a specific personality type needed to be successful in sales. Consider this: buyers also have diverse personality types. Different buyers will naturally connect with different sellers. In fact, some buyers are actually repelled by overly extroverted sales representatives. I am.

Sales representatives also differ in their general preferences and approach to sales. This is displayed in various stages of a pursuit. Some sales representatives approach sales as hunters and get energized by the thrill of the chase. They enjoy finding and connecting with new prospect and discovering the diamond in the rough. Other sales representatives are more like farmers and approach sales as a process of building and deepening relationships. Their success stems from consistency over time and networking.

Years ago I was managing a team of 10 sales representatives who were covering the southeastern states. I was concerned about how effective one representative would be, because he said bluntly that he didn't cold call—he networked. I was skeptical. You see my approach to sales was always hunting. I would find a prospect and cold call them, and I was pretty good at it. Most of the people I had known who relied on networking had sales results similar to people going into multilevel marketing efforts. They soared for a while, but once they had exhausted their personal network, their results and enthusiasm plummeted. But I was in for a lesson.

That sales representative quickly became my top performing salesperson. You see this gentleman didn't just network, he knew **how** to network. I was shown this vividly one day when he came back from a sales call. He had not only gained access to an account through networking, he had also left the meeting with the prospect's client list. What's more, the prospect had offered to introduce him to all of his clients. Wow. After that time, I began to better understand the power of leveraging individual strengths and not trying to shape people into one mold.

Sales representatives also vary in their personal knowledge, skills, and experience. In any profession, there is a certain level of core knowledge that is needed to perform your job effectively. Sales, however, is one of those professions where knowledge does not necessarily translate into success. Like a doctor with medicine, sales is practiced. This means there is a degree of trial and error. The challenge is that practice makes permanent, whether good or bad.

Based on the networking example, you can see that if I had tried to take the networking sales executive and turn him into a cold-caller, I would have hindered his personal success and the success of my team. So how do you deal with the differences and yet maintain active management on results?

MANAGING INDIVIDUALS FOR RESULTS

When anyone asks me how to manage sales individuals for results, my answer is very simple. Work backwards.

Based on both organizational and individual factors, know the level of sales that each individual needs to reach in order for his or her performance to be considered satisfactory. (Such measures are discussed later in this book.) With this information, simply begin with the end in mind. Monitor individuals' sales to date, their outstanding (decision pending) proposals, their individual performance ratios, and their pipeline. If they are performing at a level that indicates they will meet their goals, simply provide whatever assistance (support) they need. Monitor, but do not press activity level measurements. And look for ways to continue to recognize success, and encourage them to even higher performance.

If the executive's sales figures, or outstanding proposals, are weak, then move to a further examination of the opportunities in their pipeline. If the pipeline is healthy, then work with them by discussing those pursuits to see if they can move those forward.

If the pipeline is not healthy, then you must look at more granular activity level measures. Are they getting meetings? Are they making calls? Are they networking, and so on?

This approach allows sales professionals to be treated as professionals (which they prefer) and that means avoiding micromanagement, which most sales professionals abhor. Most team members take ownership of their personal results. Management is there to equip, encourage, and remove roadblocks. Only team members who are new, or who have displayed poor performance, should be managed in a direct daily or weekly manner.

DIFFERENCES CONTINUED

The value of a team is that each individual brings unique strengths to the table. These strengths benefit the team as a whole because they challenge the thought process, which fosters growth.

When I look at the differences in my sales team members, I want my team members to know what they bring to the table, which contributes to their success. In fact, I frequently ask team members, "What is it about **you**, about the way you approach your work, that makes you more successful than your peers?"

The first responses I receive are usually things like "I work hard," and so on. But I shut these down. I want them to look deeper. I ask them to think about their biggest successes, or their strongest client relationships. Why did they come about? What do they uniquely bring to the table that makes them personally successful?

It usually takes people time to be able to answer this question. Sometimes it takes days, weeks, and even months. And, for some, I never get a clear answer to the question.

Why is this so important to me?

You see, when individuals understand what it is that they uniquely bring to the table, what it is that makes them successful . . . then those individuals can **consciously** leverage that ability. They can hone it, and further sharpen it, and that talent can truly help those professionals elevate their success several fold. I have seen it happen. And so, when dealing with the differences in my team members, I look to help them identify and leverage those ingredients.

To manage sales, we must know what we are looking to achieve. This requires the use of performance measures. These performance measures, once understood, can be used to develop our goals and to manage our efforts.

PERFORMANCE MEASUREMENTS

While there are many useful measurements that can assist a sales manager in increasing sales effectiveness, I have found that the following simple ratios and measurements are key to managing your growth efforts. Here are some of the performance measurements that you should consider vital.

INITIAL MEETINGS HELD AND NEW QUALIFIED OPPORTUNITIES IDENTIFIED

This is a count of the first meeting held with new prospects during a measurement period (generally monthly and annually). *While most complex sales require several individual meetings (sales calls) with a prospect, this measure specifically only tracks the **first** meeting with a prospect on an individual purchase decision. This is important* *because it is used to calculate our conversion rate (discussed next). Only **first** meetings held with prospective clients should be counted. Meetings with clients, referral sources, networking contacts, and so on **should not** be counted in this measure.*

Generally my goal for initial meetings per month for a sales team ranges from 7–10 initial meetings per month (per professional sales representative.) Based on other performance ratios (discussed later) this level of activity should, on average, produce approximately 12–18 new clients per year for a business developer. This goal would be less for a client service professional engaged in business development activities, due to their other engagement responsibilities.

Depending on the market in which a sales representative is working, and the time they have worked within that market, finding "new" companies to call on will eventually become challenging. This being the case, I also include "new qualified opportunities" in my initial meeting count. A new qualified opportunity is an initial meeting with an existing prospect where you are discussing a new business issue that requires a separate purchase decision. Whether it is initial meetings or new qualified opportunities, we are ultimately trying to count the number of initial business conversations we are holding with prospects. By capturing this we can begin to measure our conversion rate.

CONVERSION RATE

The conversion rate is the percentage of initial sales calls that ultimately lead to a proposal. This ratio is determined by tracking the number of initial sales calls (or new qualified opportunities) with suspects or leads, and dividing that number into the total number of proposal opportunities. Proposal opportunities is the total count of current proposal requests, proposals outstanding (pending decision), as well as the count of proposals issued on previous wins and losses during the time frame measured.

Conversion rates can vary by industry, service, and even approach. I have found that within the professional services industry where I practice, a conversion rate of 33% to 50% is a good ratio when conducting general introductory meetings with prospects. When initial meetings are more targeted to a specific service, a conversion rate of 40% to 55% is a better target ratio. This demonstrates the benefit of highly targeted sales efforts, but also recognizes the place of general introductory meetings in your sales efforts.

WIN RATE (NUMBER)

The win rate (number) is the percentage of the total number of proposal opportunities that convert into a win. *This is calculated by dividing the number (count) of wins by the number (count) of proposals issued.*

Win rates are a function of solution fit, team selection, effective execution of the sales process, and competitive pressures. My expectation for win rates is to achieve a minimum of 33.3%, and my goal is to meet or exceed 50%. In highly competitive markets, this can be challenging to achieve, particularly when 5 or more competitors are bidding on a single opportunity. Mathematically in such circumstances a seller has a 20% chance of success. However, a seller who understands the buyer's decision process, and effectively executes Next Steps, can gain a competitive advantage, leading to higher win rates.

WIN RATE (DOLLARS)

The win rate (dollars) is the percentage of total dollars of proposal opportunities that convert into a Win. *This is calculated by dividing the total dollars of wins by the total dollars of proposals issued.*

Just as with win rate (number), you should strive to meet or exceed a 33-50% win rate for dollars. Measuring win rates for both the number of opportunities and dollars of opportunities over time will give sellers a better understanding of their success rate based on opportunity size. If your win rate (dollar) is consistently lower than your win rate (number), then you are finding that you are more effective with your smaller opportunities than you are with your larger ones.

COMPOSITE WIN RATE

The composite win rate is the average of win rate (number) and win rate (dollars). *This measurement is determined by adding the two rates together and dividing by two.*

Since timing and opportunity size both impact our individual win rates, using a composite (average) win rate helps balance these factors for planning purposes. My expectation for composite win rate is 33.3%, with a goal of 50% or greater.

AVERAGE SALE

Average sale is the average size of your total sales. This measurement is determined by dividing the total number (count) of sales opportunities won (new clients) into the total dollars sold.

There is no right or wrong answer for this measurement, because it is more reflective of your client base and target market. That said, this measure can potentially be influenced and increased over time by elevating your target client base, expanding your service offering, or increasing the scope of services performed. This measurement will be critical in revenue planning discussed later.

AVERAGE SALES CYCLE (WINS)

Average sales cycle (wins) is the time from pipeline entry (stage 2—Qualified prospect) to a favorable decision (stage 5—Win). *This can be easily calculated in a spreadsheet program such as Microsoft Excel by utilizing the function "Days 360" and using the pipeline entry data as the starting date, and decision date as the ending date. Averaging the resulting number for all opportunities won will provide you with your average sales cycle (wins).*

AVERAGE SALES CYCLE (LOSSES)

Similar to average sales cycle (wins), but measuring the time from pipeline entry (stage 2—Qualified prospect) to an unfavorable decision (stage 6—Loss).

Average sales cycle is often misunderstood, because it is approached too comprehensively. It is important to recognize that sales cycle is a measurement of time that does not begin until a buyer enters the Buyer's Decision Model (Window Shopping) and that continues until the time the buyer makes a decision.

Notes on sales cycle: While many people discuss the sales cycle in the accounting industry as excessively long (months or years), I have not found this to be the case. Yes, if you begin the clock when we select a company as a prospective buyer to pursue, then it may take months or years to move that company toward evaluating an opportunity for your firm to serve. However, that time is not the sales cycle. It could be considered the marketing cycle. (Remember the purpose of marketing is to build brand awareness, and to provide a positive brand experience. In doing so, you connect your targets to the people of your "brand" (firm) and in doing so, build credibility and confidence.)

In my experience, the sales cycle generally lasts 90 days or less. For my most recent sales team, sales cycle for accounts won was 72 days. Conversely, the sales cycle on our losses was approximately 119 days. This was based on approximately 248 wins on 433 pursuits over a two-year period. Knowing the spread between these two cycles helps me understand how to better manage my pipeline of activity. Like an accounts receivable aging report, you should be aware of the aging of your pipeline opportunities. Opportunities that are allowed to progress too slowly may suffer from lower success rates; therefore, they should receive more active attention.

As with any performance indicator, sales cycle is not an absolute science. Certainly there will be wins and losses that are on the far extremes of the bell curve, and judgment and discernment should be applied to all pursuits. That said, knowing that our sales cycle of losses is nearly twice as long as our sales cycle of wins should instill greater time management in us of the opportunities in the pipeline. Open opportunities that are 90 or more days out, should be reassessed to ensure that they are truly qualified and active. Therefore the pipeline should be reviewed and adjusted periodically for aging.

OTHER THOUGHTS ON PERFORMANCE RATIOS AND MEASUREMENTS

If desired, any of the statistics presented earlier can be broken down to statistics for specific teams, individuals, service areas, and so on. They also can be broken down to evaluate sales effectiveness toward opportunities of a given revenue size, industry segment, or level of decision maker (CEO, CFO, Director, etc.). Just remember that statistically you will need sufficient count of opportunities in any given segment to produce meaningful measurements.

Later in this book, we discuss the sales pipeline tool. This tool can help you track the data necessary to calculate many of the measures discussed earlier. However, it will take a reasonable amount of data in the pipeline to garner reliable measures, which may take 6 to 12 months to accumulate. In the interim, you can use target ratios.

CHAPTER
EIGHT

REVENUE PLANNING AND GOAL SETTING

The revenue planning process is actually quite simple and can be helpful in your growth efforts. Revenue planning is simply the process of examining your revenue flows in a way that helps you determine an estimated level of activity necessary to meet personal or organizational growth goals. The process of revenue planning begins with an examination of inflows and outflows of revenue.

INFLOWS AND OUTFLOWS

Let's look at it this way. In a professional services organization (CPA firm, law firm, engineering firm, etc.) annual revenue falls into one of the following categories:

Inflows of revenue (incoming revenue)
- from existing clients (annuity or recurring annual revenue)
- from existing clients (scope expansion or expansion of annual services)
- from existing clients (projects)
- from new clients (new annuity clients)
- from new clients (projects from new clients)

Outflows of revenue (lost revenue)
- from existing clients (lost annuity clients)
- from existing clients (scope retraction)
- from existing clients (projects completed last year, which will not recur)

In general, the most valuable sources of revenue for a professional services firm are those revenues that are annuity in nature. Annuity work provides the firm a revenue base that is predictable and reduces the amount of new revenue generation activity needed.

Revenue planning provides us with the ability to determine our sales objectives. The steps to do so are as follows:

1. Determine the desired revenue growth rate.
2. Assess the known losses of revenue (lost clients, completed projects, etc.).
3. Calculate your estimated percentage of lost revenue (attrition).
4. Calculate breakeven (new revenue that must be generated to replace lost revenue).
5. Calculate growth revenue (revenue needed to achieve growth goals).

6. Calculate revenue sales objective (break-even revenue + growth revenue).

Once you have calculated your revenue sales objective, you can estimate the amount of sales activity needed to achieve your growth goals.

SALES ACTIVITY PLANNING ████████████

Sales activity planning is accomplished by using the sales performance ratios discussed earlier. It is important to understand that this is a mechanical process. It is based on the assumption that all sales activity matches our calculated averages. We all know this is not the case; however, this fact does not invalidate the approach. All variances in conversion rates, win rates, and sales size, were present in the previous year as well. Taking these ratios and using them as tools is fully reasonable, and it will help us estimate the level of activity needed to achieve our growth goals. Follow these steps:

1. Start with your revenue sales objective (calculated earlier).

2. Divide your revenue sales objective by your average sales size. (This will determine number of sales needed.)

3. Divide the number of sales needed by your composite win rate percentage. (This will provide you with the number of proposals needed.)

4. Divide the number of proposals needed by your conversion rate. (This will provide you with the number of initial sales calls needed.)

Let's walk this through with some real numbers. Let's put forward the following assumptions:

A.	Firm revenue	$12,000,000
B.	Average sales size	$45,000
C.	Growth goal	10%
D.	Estimated % of lost revenue	15%
E.	Conversion rate	33%
F.	Win rate	50%

To calculate the revenue sales objective:

G.	Company revenue	$12,000,000
H.	Estimated % of lost revenue	15%
I.	Break-even revenue	$1,800,000 [$12 M x 15%]
J.	Growth revenue needed	$1,200,000 [$12 M x 10%]
K.	Revenue sales objective	$3,000,000 [$1.8 M + $1.2 M]

To calculate sales activity planning:

L.	Revenue sales objective	$3,000,000 [from K]
M.	Number of wins needed	67 [$3 M ÷ $45,000 avg. sale]
N.	Number of proposals needed	134 [67 ÷ 50% win rate]
O.	Number of pipeline opportunities	406 [134 ÷ 33% conversion rate]

These numbers seem staggering. You might ask: How can I accomplish this? This anxiety (gut check) is actually one of the strengths of performing these calculations. Developing business requires a significant investment of time and effort, and the necessary level of activity is often greatly underestimated. Goals are achievable with disciplined effort.

In this example, let's assume your firm has 8 partners, which would give each an estimated $1.5 million book of business. Let us further assume that each partner has one manager supporting his or her efforts. This would mean you would have 16 people working to accomplish the activity listed here. To meet these activity targets, each of these partners and managers would need to plan 2 initial sales calls a month, which is calculated by dividing 406 by 16 partners/managers and dividing that result by 12 months.

Suddenly, achieving these activity goals is workable (conducting 2 meetings per month per person) Even if only the partners are active in these sales efforts, then we would be looking for each partner to conduct one initial meeting per week (4 per month.) From a sales management perspective, holding each person accountable to such a goal seems doable. Doesn't it? The answer is yes, if they know that that is what it takes to achieve their organizational goals.

Important Note: When I examine the closed annual sales activity for a sales executive, and frequently for a business unit or industry group, it is very common for the two largest sales to represent 40–50% of the revenue growth (sales) for that year. I have measured this for my most recent team, and have seen this phenomenon consistently enough that I am comfortable with the following allowance.

If the activity level calculated in the example is beyond a level your organization can reasonably expect of your people, then take the activity level determined by the calculation and divide it in half. Indeed, this may be a good starting point in your first year of sales management. After the first year, assess your results. If you also find that 40–50% of your growth revenue came from your two largest sales, then you could effectively continue at this activity level. If not, then you will need to increase your activity level expectations or decrease your growth goals.

Of course, we are after more than just activity management. We want to improve our sales effectiveness. This is where practicing the use of the buyer's decision model and the discipline of sales management come together. As you increase your effectiveness at each stage of the sales process, your conversion rates increase, as do your win rates. As you become more effective, you may also be able to elevate the type of projects and clients you pursue. Each of these factors—conversion rates, win rates, and client size—have a direct impact on the level of activity necessary for achieving your growth goals. As you improve your effectiveness, you are placed in an empowering position. You can either decrease the level of activity to support your growth goals, or you can achieve greater sales growth. The decision is yours, which is a nice place to be.

Don't get me wrong; I am not unrealistic about the challenges of day-to-day business. Any number of external and internal changes can present new challenges to your growth efforts. However, by using a disciplined sales approach, you have the ability to meet those challenges directly.

GENERATING LEADS

The ability to meet your organization's sales goals is directly dependent on your initial sales call activity. This therefore requires a process for generating leads. Your professional sales executives (if you have them in your organization) can (and should) perform a portion of your lead generation function. However, I have found that the volume of lead generation activity needed organizationally usually far outstrips the capacity of your sales professionals alone.

This causes some people to consider focusing their sales executives solely on lead generation. Requiring professional sales executives to generate leads solely is not advisable for three reasons. First, professional sales executives are more valuable to you in the market in front of clients or on sales calls. Second, it is too costly to use professional sales executives as lead generators (because their salaries are generally far higher). Third, most professional sales executives that I have worked with would choose to leave the organization over time if their role was relegated to lead generation. While lead generation is an acknowledged responsibility for a business developer, a lead generation role is different from that of a professional sales executive.

For this reason, I support the use of telephone lead generators to support your business development efforts. Whether in house, or outsourced, professional telephone lead generators are able to efficiently, and cost effectively, significantly increase your lead flow leading to initial meetings. How to hire, develop, and deploy such resources is the topic of another discussion, but I think it is critically important to emphasize the need for their assistance in your organization. It will be challenging for client service professionals to generate their own leads at the level necessary to reach desired sales goals, so organizations should plan and budget around this need.

RETURN ON INVESTMENT

As we close this discussion of measurements and goal setting, I want to comment on the subject of return on investment (ROI) from your company's investment in a sales and marketing team. The areas of marketing and sales are unusual because they cover a lot of ground. Some of those areas show results that are easily measured; others do not even approach measurability. However, since the purpose of a marketing and sales department is to foster growth, it is reasonable for management to consider the return they are getting from their investment.

If your organization has a balanced marketing and sales team (meaning staff in each function) the following steps offer an easy way to assess your break-even point for your investment:

1. Calculate the total annual investment in your sales and marketing department.

2. Determine your firm's margin on revenue (% of each $ that flows to income).

3. Divide the marketing investment by the firm's margin.

The product of these steps will provide you with a rough estimate of the break-even point for your investment. At that dollar figure of sales, the firm has fully paid off its investment within a single year. Yet, I would encourage a longer ROI mindset. Here is why.

This break-even amount does not account for the lifetime value of a client to your firm. One study I read indicated that CPA firms retain clients for an average of 12 years (longer in certain industry segments). Since most of the sales of a firm are annuity in nature, this means that if a firm reached its break-even point in 1 year, then those sales for all practical purposes will pay for the department for a dozen years. I recognize this is an oversimplistic calculation. Yet it is still valid to consider because it provides you with a way of evaluating the value your marketing and sales department is bringing to your firm. With this in mind, you should be able to see how achieving the break-even point even over 2 or 3 years is still profitable to a firm over the long term. Such is the benefit of selling annuity-based work.

CHAPTER
NINE

SALES PIPELINE
MANAGEMENT

To accomplish a task both effectively and efficiently, it is generally helpful to use a tool. For a sales manager, that tool is the sales pipeline. The use of sales pipelines is not a new or unique idea. And, I would not presume to state that the pipeline process I describe here is the only way to effectively approach utilizing sales pipelines to manage your growth efforts. But I would say that sales pipelines can be and are frequently used ineffectively. So you must be thoughtful in your approach.

When understood and used properly, sales pipelines can be very effective sales and growth management tools. Unfortunately, when misunderstood, sales pipelines are not tools, but obstacles, as their management deteriorates into a mechanical and administrative process that wastes time and adds little value. With pipeline management, you tend to get one extreme or the other, with little middle ground. Because of this dichotomy, I want to take time to explain how I apply the sales pipeline within the Next Steps approach to increase sales effectiveness.

SALES PIPELINE TOOL

In its simplest form, a sales pipeline is nothing more than a list of individual sales opportunities containing key pursuit information helpful in determining next steps and in maintaining accountability.

So what does it look like? Sales pipelines are generally set up in a matrix (spreadsheet or columnar) form. Vertically, the pipeline lists each sales opportunity that an individual or team member is pursuing. Horizontally, the pipeline includes information regarding each specific pursuit.

The data points (fields) that I find most critical for a pipeline include:

- **Business unit:** Office, region, and so on
- **Sales executive or pursuit team lead:** Name
- **Pipeline entry date:** The date an opportunity is qualified and is entered into the pipeline to track. (This will be discussed further under "sales stage.")
- **Proposal issue date:** The date the proposal was delivered to the prospect
- **Decision date (win or loss):** The date you are informed of a win or loss decision
- **Prospect company:** Name
- **Objective:** The specific product or service solution you are looking to sell
- **Competitive dynamics**

- **Interpersonal dynamics**
- **Key decision criteria**
- **Constraints**
- **Risks:** A summary of the key risks discovered.
- **Next step:** A summary of your next step as determined through the STEP process.
- **Sales stage**
- **Contract Amount Estimated**
- **Contract Amount Proposed**
- **Contract Amount Wins**
- **Contract Amount Losses**

A sales pipeline is not intended to be your sole record of prospect data, it is only an extraction of the data contained in your Customer Relationship Management (CRM) system or a summary of key points from other data files. Focused and concise notes in the pipeline are sufficient for its purpose. While many of these data items are self-explanatory, a few need further explanation.

OBJECTIVE

Each sales opportunity in the pipeline should be decision based. By this I mean that when you have multiple products or services to sell to a single company, you need to examine the decision process for each product or service. If the buyer will be making one purchase decision for all the services you are offering, then only one opportunity exists (and therefore one pipeline entry). However, you may find yourself pursing work from a business where the decisions for your products or services will be made independently (either separated by time, service, or decision maker).

When decisions will be made separately, then each decision represents a different sales opportunity, and therefore each opportunity should be entered into your pipeline separately. Treating these opportunities as separate-but-related pursuits helps you better determine Next Steps for each opportunity. Each will have unique circumstances as you take the buyer through his or her decision process using the buyer's decision model.

INTERPERSONAL DYNAMICS

This data point should include your notes on any key relationships, personal dynamics, or loyalties revealed by the discovery process, which could impact the decision process. Some examples:

- "Existing provider is client's uncle."

- "CFO is alumni of competing firm."
- "Chuck's son is prospect's son's roommate at college."

KEY DECISION CRITERIA

Additional decision criteria (wants or needs) that you have been able to surface during the discovery process, which are not broadly known, or could be unique to your offering versus your competition. These are those add-on items you discovered as you worked to define the prospect's solution criteria.

CONSTRAINTS

This data point should include a summary of the key constraints you've discovered. Some examples:

- "Experiencing staffing shortages due to recent turnover."
- "New budget not set until September."
- "Only has $15,000 available for initiative."
- "Decision will require board approval."

SALES STAGE

This data point is a mechanical list of selling stages used in your CRM system and pipeline. I use the followings stages:

6   Loss

5   Win

4   Proposal delivered

3   Proposal requested

2   Qualified pursuit (for prospects in the buyer's decision model)

1   Nonqualified/Long-term pursuit (for prospects in status quo mode)

0   Do not pursue (for prospects we withdraw from pursuing or eliminate from future sales efforts)

Note: A sales pipeline is for managing qualified pursuits, not a marketing activity. Therefore, this is not the proper place to track companies you are marketing to or are targeting for lead generation activities. An opportunity should only go on the pipeline once a buyer has entered into the Buyer's Decision Model. This would be the point when you have reached a true decision maker and know that they are evaluating options to fill a want or need. Tracking general prospects in your CRM system is valuable, but it is not the purpose of the sales pipeline. Using the sales stages listed here, the pipeline should only include opportunities that are in stages 2 through 6.

CONTRACT AMOUNT

In the earlier description, four contract amount columns were listed. This structure for tracking potential sales or fees allows for quick reference and easy calculation of specific performance ratios. For any given opportunity, only one column should be utilized. Which column you use is determined by the opportunity sales stage:

- **Contract Amount Estimated:** Opportunities in stage 2 (pre-proposal)
- **Contract Amount Proposed:** Fees given in the proposal (stages 3 and 4)
- **Contract Amount Wins:** First year fees or total project fees (stage 5)
- **Contract Amount Losses:** Fee amounts proposed and lost (stage 6)

As a sales opportunity progresses, the estimated dollar fees are moved from column to column (from estimated to proposed, then from proposed to win or to loss.) Again, for any given opportunity, only one of the four columns (estimated, proposed, wins, or losses) should contain a value.

My website www.wade-clark.com offers tools to assist you with constructing a sales pipeline. I encourage you to access this information. Pay particular attention to the upcoming topic "Prospective Pipeline."

A template for the pipeline described is also available for free download at www.wade-clark.com.

USING THE SALES PIPELINE

By providing a way to track the performance ratios mentioned earlier, a sales pipeline allows you to assess your progress toward your sales objectives. It will also provide you with the ability to quickly review individual sales opportunities for progress. When possible, I recommend holding pipeline discussions with your sales team monthly.

When holding pipeline discussions, you will find that the tool provides you with an efficient basis. Since all pursuit information is consolidated in one location, a quick glance will provide you with an understanding of what areas of discovery are left to perform on each pursuit. Those data points will show up as blank fields on the pipeline. You will also be able to spot trends, indicating areas where a given sales executive may need further training, development, or focus.

I have frequently seen pipelines where a sales executive has diligently "filled out" information. But a review of the information clearly shows that the sales executive doesn't fully understand what he or she really needs to accomplish with that discovery point. For example, the field Solution Criteria may state: "low price, quality service." While I will not debate that a client wants quality service at a good price, this statement does not tell us anything that we would not otherwise know.

This field should indicate criteria (wants or needs) that we have been able to discover, that go beyond the initial core needs. These are decision factors our competition has likely not uncovered. Factors like—"client would like staff training on the methodology," or "client would like to receive periodic benchmarking against their industry." Unique findings like these provide us with differentiation against our competition. And differentiation helps improve win rates.

The field Constraints may state "low price." What does this really mean? First, do we know this, or is it an assumption? If we know this, what is the prospect's budget tolerance? Are there variables that could impact the budget, such as timing? Depending on the service, would they be willing to do some work internally in exchange for a lower price?

When fields are filled out generically, it frequently indicates that the topic was not actually talked about in depth with the client or that we did not take those discussions down to specifics. We must address specifics, not generalities.

PROSPECTIVE PIPELINE ███████████████

One of the key calculations I use to assess the strength of a sales executive's pipeline is a measurement I call "prospective pipeline." The prospective pipeline is a useful measure because it provides me with a way to gauge the overall health of a sales executive's activities based on that executive's statistical performance over time.

Essentially the prospective pipeline measure gives me an estimate of the total dollar amount of sales that I can predict for that specific sales executive (or business unit), from all sales activity that is currently in their pipeline.

Calculate the prospective pipeline measure as follows:

1. Calculate (separately) the total (sum) of the following pipeline columns
   - a. Contract Amount Estimate (opportunities at stage 2)
   - b. Contract Amount Proposed (opportunities at stages 3 & 4)
2. Multiply the total of 1.a. "Contact Amount Estimate" by the sales executives conversion rate (This provides an estimate of qualified opportunities that may move over time to proposal.)
3. Add this amount (#2) to the total of 1.b. "Contract Amount Proposed." (This provides you an estimate of total proposals from all qualified pursuits over time.)
4. Multiply the amount calculated in #3 by the sales executive's composite win rate. (The result is your "prospective pipeline" amount.)

Most pipeline measurements I have seen used (and incorporated into most CRM systems) base their estimates of prospective sales on the stage that an opportunity is in based on a given sales process. For example, they make an assumption that if an opportunity is at a certain stage, then there is an x% chance of that opportunity becoming a win.

My experience has shown me that no two sales opportunities are the same, regardless of the sales stage they are in. In addition, I have found that different sales executives, and business units, consistently have different results from their pursuits.

The power of the prospective pipeline figure is that it measures total pipeline activity against that specific sales executive's (or business unit's) historical sales performance. I find using this approach provides me with a much better assessment (predictor) of the health of their pipeline.

The practical application of this measure is as follows. I require my sales executives to build their pipeline to the point where their "prospective pipeline" measure equals or exceeds their annual sales goal. By doing so, the sales executive will have the highest likelihood of achieving their annual sales quotas consistently over time.

Additionally, sales executives (or business units) will need to work to maintain their prospective pipeline at or above their annual sales goals. This is necessary because the prospective pipeline measurement is reduced any time a proposal opportunity is finalized with either a win, or a loss.

CHAPTER
TEN

GROWTH MANAGEMENT

STRATEGIC CONSIDERATIONS

Almost all of your proactive sales efforts should be focused on the key industries or services areas where your firm is looking to build a strong strategic position. This means that your efforts should start slow and be progressive. They will accelerate over time as your resume grows in a given area. Unfortunately, this is often a challenge for many firms. Partners and Sales representatives may say they want to specialize or focus on a given area. But when you examine their efforts, they are all over the board. This is because they don't want to turn down any opportunity because they feel they are limiting their growth efforts.

Remember, when you decided to focus on an area, you are at the same time deciding **not** to focus on other areas. From a long-term perspective, this is the best course of action, but it is an area I seem to battle constantly.

Firms that understand the strength of this focus, over time, enjoy much higher success rates in their areas of specialty. Firms that don't understand get frustrated because they are treating their sales efforts as one-time pursuits, and their lower win rates reflect this error. And perhaps the biggest error of all is the idea of chasing the proverbial "low-hanging fruit."

THE ALMOST-MYTH OF LOW-HANGING FRUIT

Most people have certain things that frustrate them professionally. For me, one of those items is the use of the term low-hanging fruit. This term continually comes up in companies with which I have work. The premise is fairly straightforward—focus time on finding those areas where there is great opportunity and few obstacles. It is usually accompanied by the sage phrase, "We must work smarter, not harder." This premise assumes that we can gain quick advantage and secure work quickly. However, in my opinion, the premise is based on a flawed assumption that there is a good amount of excellent, **easy-to-obtain** client work that is just ripe for the picking.

In my opinion, the search for low-hanging fruit is largely a futile quest—one that is not much different from Don Quixote charging at windmills. Don't get me wrong. I do believe there are indeed areas of low-hanging fruit. But it is not found in the context (the places or situations) in which this term is most often used. We will get to this in a moment. For now, I think it would be helpful to explain my concerns related to this quest for low-hanging fruit.

SIMPLIFYING COMPLEX SALES

UNKNOWN "QUALITY" PROSPECTS

When selecting good prospects to secure as clients, most firms look for companies that are well run, produce a quality product or service, are profitable, and have a strong management team. Often their executive team members are well connected and influential and are active in the community. Businesses of this quality have a good reputation in the marketplace, so it is logical to assume your competitors will be aware of them. Therefore it is rare to find such companies that are relatively unknown.

PEOPLE BECOME OPPORTUNISTIC, NOT STRATEGIC

When you are chasing the proverbial low-hanging fruit, you are in essence choosing to be opportunistic, not strategic. Your frame of reference becomes shortsighted as you work to be at the right place at the right time. This short-term focus is damaging for two reasons. First, it is an inefficient and ineffective prospecting approach. You must rely on securing business from companies in which you have little to no corporate knowledge or relationships. Second, this opportunistic approach leads to securing suboptimal clients. You end up gaining work from companies that may indeed have a need, but that do not match your desired client profile. Unfortunately, you can't afford to pass up the work because you don't have better opportunities in the wings. This increases your risk.

It is important to be strategic about your business development efforts, this means commitment over time, not short-term thinking. When you are strategic, you can shape the future of your business by securing clients that will be best for your company for the long haul. It is the difference between investing and gambling. You may be able to show some successes in short-term gambling, but the wise investor who is selective and patient will in the long-term reap the greater rewards.

ASSUMING YOUR COMPETITION HAS BEEN PASSIVE

Frequently when people talk about going after the low-hanging fruit, it is at a time when they have "woken up" and decide to be more proactive with their business development efforts. Since **they** have not been diligent pursuing strategic prospects over time, they conclude that they should be efficient with their time and focus on low-hanging fruit. The problem with this logic is that it assumes your competition also has been passive in its sales and marketing efforts. In today's competitive environment, this is a naive perspective. You should always assume your competition is, and has been, actively pursuing your strategic targets (*and* your clients).

WHERE IS LEGITIMATE LOW-HANGING FRUIT?

There are two areas where you can find legitimate low-hanging fruit. The first is expansion of services with existing clients. Some call this cross-selling. Your clients likely have needs that you are not addressing. You have already gained their trust and demonstrated your ability to serve them well. Therefore it is a wise thing to take time to discuss their greater needs on a regular basis; presenting the solution you can provide to meet those needs. In this way, you are able to expand your revenue base and deepen your client relationship and trust.

The second legitimate area of low-hanging fruit is in situations where you can be first, or early, to market. When you can enter the market for a service early in its life cycle, you have an opportunity to capture market share. Companies will be cautious but interested in new products or approaches, so you can open doors, which before may have been closed to your company.

Both of these areas of low-hanging fruit can indeed be profitable and have strong long-term strategic impact on your business. As a sales manager, it is your responsibility to help keep your organization and your sales executives focused on those efforts that will produce the best long-term benefits. Therefore, be sure to really examine what people mean when they say low-hanging fruit. Are they recommending activity that in the long-term interest of your business is strategic, efficient, and effective, or are they just being opportunistic or lazy. Remember, some fruit that is easy to reach can be rotten.

In Closing

It is my genuine hope that this book has provided you with new knowledge and understanding in the area of sales and growth management. I even further hope that it has given you some tools that you can use to help your buyers make wise purchase decisions and to improve your sales success.

SO WHAT IS YOUR NEXT STEP?

I would encourage you to read this book more than once because the concepts (though simple) take some time to take root. Once they are ingrained in your thinking, you will find the simplicity of the process to be very powerful.

I also invite you to visit www.wade-clark.com. On this site you will find tools, such as the sales pipeline template, available for download. You will also find a blog and discussion board. I welcome you to share your successes, insights, and questions on the discussion board. This is a work in process, and we are all learning together. I welcome you to join the community as we grow together. If I can assist your firm with its growth challenges, please visit www.newvisionadvisors.com. I wish you the best in your sales efforts.

CPSIA information can be obtained at www.ICGtesting.com
Printed in the USA
LVOW101408010712

288331LV00003B/4/P